Alfred, Lord Tennyson

CURRENTLY AVAILABLE

BLOOM'S MAJOR WORLD POETS

Geoffrey Chaucer

Emily Dickinson

John Donne

T. S. Eliot

Robert Frost

Langston Hughes

John Milton

Edgar Allan Poe

Shakespeare's Poems & Sonnets

Alfred, Lord Tennyson

Walt Whitman

William Wordsworth

BLOOM'S MAJOR SHORT STORY WRITERS

William Faulkner

F. Scott Fitzgerald

Ernest Hemingway

O. Henry

James Joyce

Herman Melville

Flannery O'Connor

Edgar Allan Poe

J. D. Salinger

John Steinbeck

Mark Twain

Eudora Welty

Alfred, Lord Tennyson

BLOOM'S

MAJOR

POETS

EDITED AND WITH AN INTRODUCTION
BY HAROLD BLOOM

© 1999 by Chelsea House Publishers, a division of Main Line Book Co.

Introduction © 1999 by Harold Bloom

Printed and bound in the United States of America.

First Printing
1 3 5 7 9 8 6 4 2

Library of Congress Cataloging-in-Publication Data

Tennyson, Alfred, Baron, 1809-1892.
Alfred, Lord Tennyson / edited and with an introduction by Harold Bloom.
p.   cm. — (Bloom's major poets)
Includes bibliographical references and index.
ISBN 0-7910-5112-9 (hc)
1. Tennyson, Alfred Tennyson, Baron, 1809-1892—Criticism and
interpretation—Handbooks, manuals, etc.   2. Tennyson, Alfred
Tennyson, Baron, 1809-1892—Examinations—Study guides.   3. English
poetry—Themes, motives—Handbooks, manuals, etc.   I. Bloom, Harold.
II. Title.   III. Series.
PR5588.T39   1998
821'8—dc21
98-49210
CIP

Chelsea House Publishers
1974 Sproul Road, Suite 400
Broomall, PA 19008-0914

Contributing Editor: Janyce Marsen

Contents

User's Guide

This volume is designed to present biographical, critical, and bibliographical information on the author's best-known or most important poems. Following Harold Bloom's editor's note and introduction is a detailed biography of the author, discussing major life events and important literary accomplishments. A thematic and structural analysis of each poem follows, tracing significant themes, patterns, and motifs in the work.

A selection of critical extracts, derived from previously published material from leading critics, analyzes aspects of each poem. The extracts consist of statements from the author, if available, early reviews of the work, and later evaluations up to the present. A bibliography of the author's writings (including a complete list of all books written, cowritten, edited, and translated), a list of additional books and articles on the author and the work, and an index of themes and ideas in the author's writings conclude the volume.

~

Harold Bloom is Sterling Professor of the Humanities at Yale University and Henry W. and Albert A. Berg Professor of English at the New York University Graduate School. He is the author of over 20 books and the editor of more than 30 anthologies of literary criticism.

Professor Bloom's works include *Shelley's Mythmaking* (1959), *The Visionary Company* (1961), *Blake's Apocalypse* (1963), *Yeats* (1970), *A Map of Misreading* (1975), *Kabbalah and Criticism* (1975), and *Agon: Toward a Theory of Revisionism* (1982). *The Anxiety of Influence* (1973) sets forth Professor Bloom's provocative theory of the literary relationships between the great writers and their predecessors. His most recent books include *The American Religion* (1992), *The Western Canon* (1994), *Omens of Millennium: The Gnosis of Angels, Dreams, and Resurrection* (1996), and *Shakespeare: The Invention of the Human* (1998).

Professor Bloom earned his Ph.D. from Yale University in 1955 and has served on the Yale faculty since then. He is a 1985 MacArthur Foundation Award recipient and served as the Charles Eliot Norton Professor of Poetry at Harvard University in 1987–88. He is currently the editor of other Chelsea House series in literary criticism, including BLOOM'S NOTES, BLOOM'S MAJOR SHORT STORY WRITERS, MAJOR LITERARY CHARACTERS, MODERN CRITICAL VIEWS, MODERN CRITICAL INTERPRETATIONS, and WOMEN WRITERS OF ENGLISH AND THEIR WORKS.

Editor's Note

My Introduction comments briefly upon all six poems studied in this volume, and emphasizes Tennyson's elegiac mastery.

The critical extracts are copious, and I will mention only a few high points here. Herbert F. Tucker and Christopher Ricks illuminate "The Lady of Shalott," while "Ulysses" is analyzed by Tony Robbins in regard both to its Homeric and Dantesque backgrounds.

"Locksley Hall"'s Byronism is examined by Claude de L. Ryals, while Traci Gardner establishes the poem's mythic backgrounds.

Cleanth Brooks's famous analysis of "Tears, Idle Tears" contrasts with J. Hillis Miller's deconstruction of the lyric.

Morte d'Arthur is compared to its sources in Malory by Herbert Tucker, after which *In Memoriam* receives an influential tribute from T. S. Eliot. John D. Rosenberg and Donald S. Hair also provide useful insights into Tennyson's masterwork.

Introduction

HAROLD BLOOM

As a lyric and elegiac poet, Tennyson has few rivals in the English language. That he reflects the main movement of mind and morals of his era is also part of his permanent importance. In English poetry, Tennyson is the mediating figure between John Keats and the Pre-Raphaelites, and the Aesthetic Movement after them. Tennyson's acute, almost morbid sensibility, his power over language, and his uncanny ear also made him (together with Walt Whitman) the true precursor of T. S. Eliot. Eliot preferred to station his forebearers elsewhere, in medieval Italy and in nineteenth-century France, but *The Waste Land* is very much the phantasmagoric mode that Tennyson manifested in *Maud* and in the *Idylls of the King.*

"The Lady of Shalott" helped form not only the style of Pre-Raphaelite poetry, but also engendered Poe's most characteristic lyrics. Elaine, "the lily maid of Astolat" (Shalott) is a visionary who comes under the curse of the image of Sir Lancelot, with whom she falls in love. In an extraordinary fantasia, the white-robed Lady floats down the river to Camelot, in a boat bearing her own name. In the poignant final stanza (not much admired by feminist critics) this strange fable ends with a reflection by Lancelot that leaves us musing as to what might have been:

> But Lancelot mused a little space;
> He said, 'She has a lovely face;
> God in his mercy lend her grace,
>   The Lady of Shalott'

A different Tennyson is heard in the sublime dramatic monologue "Ulysses," a subtle, equivocal poem, which on one level is a resolute elegy for Tennyson's best friend, Arthur Henry Hallam. Yet the Ulysses of the poem is not the Homeric Ulysses, but Dante's Ulysses, who is in Hell for evil counsel (though Dante clearly admires him nevertheless). Tennyson is of many minds toward Ulysses in this poem; the hero-villain is a High-Romantic quester attempting to go beyond the limits of knowledge. And yet Ulysses loves no one, scorns his son's sense of responsibility, and desires only his own destiny:

> Though much is taken, much abides, and though
> We are not now that strength which in old days
> Moved earth and heaven; that which we are, we are;
> One equal temper of heroic hearts,
> Made weak by time and fate, but strong in will
> To strive, to seek, to find, and not to yield.

Ulysses here echoes Milton's Satan, but Satan at his most heroic: "And what is else not to be overcome?" The heroic accents of Tennyson's Ulysses contrast sharply with the ranting tone of the morbid youth who speaks "Locksley Hall," which nevertheless remains a permanently popular poem. The beautiful Virgilian lyric "Tears, Idle Tears" continues to be even more popular, with its wonderful elegiac accents:

> Dear as remembered kisses after death,
> And sweet as those by hopeless fancy feigned
> On lips that are for others; deep as love,
> Deep as first love, and wild with regret;
> O Death in Life, the days that are no more.

This is as universal a mourning as Virgil and Wordsworth invoke. Tennyson laments again the death of Hallam in the majestic *Morte d'Arthur*, where the dying King Arthur speaks a wisdom as memorable as it is paradoxical:

> The old order changeth, yielding place to new,
> And God fulfills Himself in many ways,
> Lest one good custom should corrupt the world.

The summit of Tennyson is the complete *In Memoriam*, a long lyric cycle that gathers together every element in his elegiac art. It should be read straight through, although scores of the individual poems have their own perfection. T. S. Eliot particularly admired Poem VII, "Dark house by which once more I stand." My own favorite is Poem CIII, in which Tennyson has a vision of a resurrected Hallam, and sails off with him into another realm:

> And while the wind began to sweep
>   A music out of sheet and shroud,
>   We steered her toward a crimson cloud
> That landlike slept along the deep.

Tennyson, though somewhat out of fashion at this time, will return in the new century. Masters of lyric and elegy are infrequent; only W. B. Yeats, in the century now dying, was Tennyson's peer. ❁

Biography of
Alfred, Lord Tennyson

(1809–1892)

Alfred, Lord Tennyson, born in 1809, was to achieve what so many other poets and writers throughout the centuries were unable to achieve—fame and success during his lifetime. Indeed, in 1850, after the publication of *In Memoriam*, Tennyson was to become England's poet laureate, a public office bestowed upon one who has not only distinguished himself by his work to date, but one who is also honored with the appointed responsibility of representing the state during its most solemn and celebratory occasions. The poet laureateship also carried with it an annual stipend and, to the financially beleaguered poet, provided a most welcome advantage to his political appointment. However, notwithstanding this honor, Tennyson was to remain modest about this appointment throughout the rest of his life. As Christopher Ricks states in his biography, *Tennyson*, "[I]t was not an honor about which he ever became self-important," rather, it occasioned a self-effacing posture that would cause Tennyson to underrate his own abilities to live up to the task. "In fact, he was to find a great deal that was very congenial (not taskwork at all) in the Queen's hopes for him . . . The Queen herself he was to thank with dignity." "Revered, beloved," Tennyson's first publication as Poet Laureate, expresses both his gratitude to Victoria and his own humbleness for the honor granted him. "Take, Madam, this poor book of song; /For though the faults were thick as dust / In vacant chambers, I could trust / Your kindness."

To many of his contemporaries, Tennyson's life was one of ease and good fortune, marred only by the early loss of his best friend. However, despite this reputation, Tennyson was well-acquainted with pain and emotional turmoil. He grew up in a parsonage, but his family life was neither serene nor religious; in fact, it was full of tumult and instability.

He was the fourth in a family of twelve children, many of whom suffered from a variety of emotional and character disorders, drug addiction, and familial dissension. One of Alfred's brothers, Edward, had to be confined to an insane asylum. Another brother, Charles, exhibited early poetic talent and creativity and even earned the praise of the great poet Samuel Coleridge, but he could not handle the depressions to which he was subject; he escaped his melancholy through opium addiction. The most dramatic of Alfred's brothers was Frederick, suspended from Cambridge University for disobedience and impertinence, who quarreled violently with their father. Indeed, in a letter written by their mother to her father-in-law, Mrs. Tennyson asserts that her husband, armed with a knife and loaded gun, had intended to stab Frederick in the jugular vein.

The enmity between Frederick and his father was so bitter and fierce that it caused his parent's separation. In February 1819, Mrs. Tennyson wrote a letter reciting all the humiliation and abuse to which she and her children had been subjected, describing the desperate feelings that caused her to abandon her marriage so precipitously: "I remonstrated with him as having such dangerous weapons and told him he would be killing himself—he said he should not do this but he would kill others and Frederick should be one." Despite Dr. George Tennyson's denial of any implicit suicidal tendencies in his personality, there is incontrovertible evidence that he was bent on self-destruction.

For all his emotional instability, Alfred's father, the Reverend Dr. George Tennyson, was a man of learning. He owned a considerable library, played the harp, and even wrote some poetry of his own. As a spiritual guide, however, he was wanting, too crippled by the pain caused by his own father's harsh judgment and cruel behavior.

Dr. Tennyson (Alfred's father) had suffered the misfortune of being disinherited by his own father, in favor his brother Charles. The clerical profession was forced upon Dr. Tennyson when he was cut off from his rightful inheritance and means of financial support. In 1820, Dr. Tennyson wrote to his father: "You have long injured me by your suspicions . . . . God judge between you and me. You make and have always made a false estimate of me in every respect." Unable to reconcile the bitter rift with his father, Dr. Tennyson's bitterness drove him to become an abusive alcoholic. Thus, the sins of the fathers were to be visited upon the next generation of sons, of whom Alfred was one.

In sum, to say the very least, Alfred had an unhappy and unstable childhood, the details of which account for many of the most prevalent themes throughout his works: issues such as suicide, the lifelong quest for some compensatory relief for the loss and pain of childhood, and a fascination with the literature of a very distant past, most notably, the Arthurian legend as narrated by Sir Thomas Malory.

Nonetheless, for all the expressions of doom and failure in Tennyson and his invocation of the Arthurian legend to express that grief, there is always, at the very same time, a way out of those terrible predicaments. The relief and hope for a better future resides in every poem, including some of the darker ones presented here, such as "Tears, Idle Tears" and "The Lady of Shalott." That hope is nothing other than finding a new way to explain and then convince ourselves that happier days will return. Thus, consolation is contained in language; it springs from our ability to refashion our understanding of otherwise irremediable pain and sorrow.

Alfred had used his gift for language to deal with emotional pain in this way even before he left his family home. He had even published a volume of poetry with his brother Charles. Once he went to Cambridge, this talent of his drew the attention of a group of gifted students who called themselves the "Apostles." They encouraged Alfred to devote his life to poetry, and thus language provided the path that helped him to escape from his unhappy childhood.

Up until then, he had known scarcely anyone outside his own family's dysfunctional circle. He was tall and powerfully built, but he was painfully shy; the literary friendships he formed at Cambridge helped him to gain a new confidence in himself and his abilities. The most important of these friendships was with Arthur Hallam, a prominent Apostle who later became engaged to Alfred's sister. Hallam's sudden death in 1833 threatened to overwhelm Alfred, but as always he used poetry as a means to deal with emotional pain. Not only *In Memoriam*, the long elegy written in honor of Hallam, but many of Tennyson's other poems as well give tribute to Hallam and his early influence on Alfred's life.

Alfred was forced to leave Cambridge because of family problems and financial difficulties. He returned home and devoted himself to studying and practicing the craft of poetry. His early works were attacked by critics as being "obscure" or "affected," and while Tennyson agonized over these criticisms, he also profited from them. His talent continued to mature, and in 1850 he at last achieved fame and success with the publication of *In Memoriam*.

That was the same year in which he replaced another great poet, William Wordsworth, as the poet laureate of England. He was also, finally, able to achieve his long postponed marriage to Emily Sellwood, with whom he had fallen in love in 1836. From that point on, Tennyson was able to support his family and purchase a home in the country, where he could enjoy the seclusion of which he so often wrote in his poems. He gained a reputation as a colorful character, a huge, gruff, shaggy man who read his poetry in a booming voice.

Tennyson died in 1892, having achieved the greatest happiness of all: to live as he pleased, a man of great social vision who commented on the issues of his times, a character who spoke for a nation. He was buried at Westminster Abbey, along with so many of his great literary forebears. ❀

Thematic Analysis of
"The Lady of Shalott"

Originally written in 1832 and published in final form in 1842, "The Lady of Shalott" is a very strange and tautly rendered poem, consisting of a series of "gnomic verses"—short, tightly constructed statements of general truths. Likewise, its structure is both compact and highly artistic, blending sight and sound to evoke strong feelings of loneliness and seclusion in a remote and magical past. The beauty of its own artistry implies that the poem is also concerned with the problem of artistic isolation, an issue which can lead to some contradictory interpretations—for instance whether the seclusion necessary for artistic achievement runs counter to the need for daily interaction with the outside world and whether the life of peaceful retirement is preferable to the life of active involvement. These issues cannot be resolved in any easy or straightforward manner.

Nevertheless, despite the difficulty in pinning down any clear-cut resolutions within Tennyson's gloomy portrait of the kingdom of Camelot, "The Lady of Shalott" was a very popular poem in its own time. Tennyson stated that the source for "The Lady of Shalott" was derived from an Italian romance about the Donna di Scalotta, and it was not, as was generally believed at the time of publication, based upon the story of the maid of Astolat in Malory's *Morte d'Arthur.* Nevertheless, because the poem contains so many trappings which are an inherent part of the Arthurian legend—the magical kingdom of Camelot, Lancelot's bejeweled armor, and the barge that ferries the dying Lady, as well as the very name Shalott, which appears to be an anagram of the maid of Astolat (a rearrangement of the letters of a word to produce another word or meaning)—readers immediately identified this poem's setting as Arthurian.

Indeed, when this seemingly apparent source is denied by the poet himself, readers are left feeling even more disoriented. The poem's obscure setting is like an echo to its illusive meaning. The poem is truly a well guarded room in an impenetrable tower: "Four gray walls, and four gray towers, / Overlook a space of flowers, / And the silent isle imbowers, The Lady of Shalott."

Part I of the poem places the reader on the island of Shalott, where there are a series of sharp contrasts between the interior of the tower and the busy world outside. "On either side the river lie / Long fields of barley and of rye, / That clothe the wold and meet the sky." The outside world is ripe with vegetation, fields of barley and rye. However, juxtaposed to these strong images of nature and vitality, are images of artistic and sexual purity symbolized by the lilies, the only flowers of which we are told. "And up and down the people go, / Gazing where the lilies blow." Thus, an immediate tension is created between activity and seclusion, art versus life, and passion versus a paralysis of emotion.

Likewise, Camelot is placed by the river, which traditionally symbolizes life, purposeful movement, progress, and a means of communicating and interacting with the rest of the world. Thus, the inhabitants of Camelot have the means to interact even beyond the confines of their own kingdom while the isle is deaf to the lady's existence. She is imprisoned within the tower and the conditions of that imprisonment render her paralyzed and immobile.

However, despite her divorce from the external world, the inhabitants of Camelot also have a curious awareness of the Lady's existence, though she is known only by virtue of her voice. "Only reapers, reaping early / . . . Hear a song that echoes cheerly / From the river winding clearly." The lady is thus ethereal and remote rather than a real person.

The reapers, weary from hard labor, further underscore the unreality of the artist who has traditionally, if unfairly, been seen as one far removed from the concerns of the workaday world and the physical labor required to earn one's keep. In sharp contrast to weary reapers and heavy barges, the Lady is referred to as a "fairy." Finally, with respect to the question of artistic isolation, and despite the negative implications of a life of retirement, the island of Shalott can also be understood as a safe haven for artists.

Part II begins by telling us that the Lady is living under an evil yet vague threat on her life and thus offers an immediate and compelling explanation as to why the Lady has been forced to accept a permanent alienation from the real world. If she dares to look upon that world, a curse will fall upon her: "There she weaves by night and day / A magic web with colors gay. / She has heard a whisper say, / A curse is on her if she stay/ To look down to Camelot." Unlike the legendary kingdom, the Camelot she is forbidden to know represents the real world. Nevertheless, she cheerfully accepts her isolation and becomes completely focused on her work. The perfection of her weaving is all that matters to her. "She knows not what the curse may be, / And so she weaveth steadily, / And little other care hath she, / The Lady of Shalott."

But in spite of her "cheery" acceptance of her plight, the issue remains: the Lady is removed from the real world. Her only knowledge of reality comes from reflections in the mirror at which she looks for both the accuracy and perfection of her work and for knowledge of the world outside her room. "And moving thro' a mirror clear / That hangs before her all the year, / Shadows of the world appear." Her art is, indeed, not a reflection of nature but is relegated to being a shadow of a shadow, with the Lady merely a spectator, removed from life.

As distant as she is, the Lady cannot be involved in social causes, an involvement which became increasingly important to the poets and artists of the Victorian period. She only knows of love and knightly adventures, spirituality, the natural world, and the politics of the life at court, but she is not vitally connected to any of it. "Sometimes a curly shepherd-lad, / Or long-hair'd page in crimson clad, / Goes by to tower'd Camelot . . . She hath no loyal knight and true, / The Lady of Shalott."

What is even more poignant about her existence is that up until now she has believed her art to be a satisfying compensation for the active life. "But in her web she still delights / To weave the mirror's magic sights." That satisfaction, however, is soon to be undermined when she sees reflected in the mirror a funeral and a wedding, two important markers of the human life cycle from which she has been precluded. The funeral foreshadows the fate she will later suffer when she violates the proscription placed upon her and gazes directly upon the world outside her window.

Her protective isolation is first ruptured through her partial recognition of the consequences of her existence. She sees her seclusion as a type of illness, exclaiming that "I am half sick of shadows." Indeed, when she has been so far cut off from the rest of the world, we should not expect her to be capable of anything more than a partial awareness of her situation.

Having begun to tire of her situation in Part II, Part III begins with an intensification of images and feelings for the world she has so long been denied. Here she finally gazes upon the imposing Sir Lancelot, a knight who has experienced great adventures and who is fully engaged with the most exciting aspects of life. "He rode between the barley-sheaves. The sun came dazzling thro the leaves, / And flamed upon the brazen greaves / Of bold Sir Lancelot." The strong images used to describe Lancelot, "the gemmy bridle glitter'd free," suggest a life full of passion, love, and adventure, in sharp contrast to the emotionally paralyzed life to which the Lady of Shalott has been condemned.

Her first awareness of Lancelot is from the mirror: "From the bank and from the river / He flash'd into the crystal mirror," and it is his presence which is so compelling that it shoots "a bearded meteor, trailing light." That irrepressible energy, which at first only "suggests" the transformation of her static life into a life-affirming gesture of passion, is met by the Lady's initial resistance to the temptation of the imposing figure of Lancelot. What breaks the paralysis is Lancelot's chosen medium of song as the means to communicate with the Lady. "'Tirra lirra,' by the river / Sang Sir Lancelot."

Song is a medium familiar to the Lady, but now she realizes, for the first time, that singing exists in the world outside her window. The temptation now becomes irresistible. The Lady leaves her weaving, forgets the curse, and gazes with her own eyes upon the world of Camelot.

The threatened curse now manifests itself when the web disappears and the mirror, which until the breaking of the spell was her only source of knowledge of the outside world, cracks, signaling the end of her artistic abilities. "Out flew the web and floated wide; / The mirror crack'd from side to side; / 'The curse is come upon me,' cried / The Lady of Shalott."

We, the readers, are here left with this ironic turn of events: the Lady's act of responding to Lancelot, reaching out to the sensual attractions of life in the external world, at the very same time is the end of any possible fulfillment of these newly awakened desires. The impulse to live contains its own death sentence.

Until now, the outside world has been rendered in lush and passionate colors: "All in the blue unclouded weather / Thick-jewell'd shone the saddle-leather." But once the Lady moves toward that life, the brilliance begins to fade and nature dons a gray and gloomy façade. "In the stormy east-wind straining, / The pale yellow woods were waning, / The broad stream in his banks complaining."

Thus, she is forever denied the experience of an active and passionate involvement with the world. The moment of her being reawakened is also the moment of her death, and she must leave Camelot, wrapped in a white funeral shroud that simultaneously symbolizes her death and her innocence of the world, the same shadowy, insubstantial state that has marked her entire existence. Her first attempt to grasp hold of life is at the very same time her letting go. "She loosed the chain, and down she lay / The broad stream bore her far away, / The Lady of Shalott."

And, as the Lady of Shalott floats away, "[s]inging in her song she died," we understand, even if we do not wish to accept, the irresolvable conflict in "The Lady of Shalott"—that the end of artistic isolation leads to the death of creativity. The artist's intense loneliness is absolutely necessary, for all great art demands solitude and silent reflection. ❀

Critical Views on
"The Lady of Shalott"

[F.E.L. Priestly has edited an edition of William Godwin's *Enquiry Concerning Political Justice and Its Influence on Morals and Happiness.* In the excerpt below from his book *Language and Structure in Tennyson's Poetry*, Priestly discusses "The Lady of Shalott" in the context of Tennyson's so-called period of silence, 1832–1842, in which he made extensive revisions to his work, and concludes that the moody landscape of this particular poem benefited greatly by bringing a visual unity to the contrast between inside and outside worlds.]

The ten years between the publication of the 1832 volume and that of the two volumes of *Poems* in 1842, which finally established Tennyson's reputation firmly, used to be called the ten years of silence. There was a popular impression that the unfriendly reception of the earlier volumes had so discouraged the poet that he went through a period of inactivity before he could bring himself back with confidence to his task of writing. The truth is that the ten years were very active ones, in which Tennyson was not only doing a great deal of new writing, but revising, often radically, the earlier poems which still seemed promising to him. The nature of the revisions is most interesting, since in general they show a new or vastly increased awareness of the necessity of total shape and structure in a poem. . . .

Perhaps the most radical, and certainly one of the most amazingly successful, is the surgery he performed on *The Lady of Shalott.* Some of the revisions made in this poem for 1842 are purely tonal: Tennyson particularly referred to 'kicking the geese out of the boat', that is, reducing the hissing sibilants, especially adjacent ones. In the original second stanza, for example, he wrote

Willows whiten, aspens shiver
The sun beam-showers break and quiver
In the stream that runneth ever.

There are eight sibilants in the three lines. The revised version neatly transposes 'shiver' and 'quiver', subdues the emphatic sibilants of 'sunbeam-showers' to the muted 'Little breezes dusk and shiver' (brilliantly improving the image at the same time) and puts 'wave' in place of 'stream'. . . .

The original opening stanza had set up a brilliant contrast between the colour and movement of the world outside, where road and river run down to Camelot, and 'up and down the people go,' and the cold immobility of the 'Four gray walls, and four gray towers' of the 'silent isle'. But this powerful effect is blurred in the 1832 text by the detail that follows. The reaper, in 1832, 'hears *her* ever chanting cheerly, Like an angel, singing clearly'. In 1842, the reapers only hear a *song*. And the description of the island quoted above, which was followed by a sharply detailed description of the Lady:

> A pearl garland winds her head:
> She leaneth on a velvet bed,
> Fully royally apparellèd . . .

is now removed. In place of the rich visual detail which, by allowing us to see the Lady and her bower as vividly and as clearly as the outside world, destroyed the contrast and fused her and her island into visual unity with the outside, we now have three rhetorical questions, to all of which the answer is the same:

> But who hath seen her wave her hand?
> Or at the casement seen her stand?
> Or is she known in all the land,
>   The Lady of Shalott?

She is now a legend and a voice, unseen, unknown. The reaper cannot know that he hears *her* voice: he hears a *voice* and attributes it to 'the fairy Lady'. The towers now stand in their grayness, overlooking a space of flowers, but the island itself is no longer a place itself of colour and growth, 'over-trailed with roses'. No one sees any sign of life there, the shallop flits by 'unhailed'; there is only that mysterious song heard by the reapers. . . .

The final stanza . . . is replaced by an absolute triumph:

> Who is this? and what is here?
> And in the lighted palace near
> Died the sound of royal cheer;
> And they crossed themselves for fear,
>   All the knights of Camelot:
> But Lancelot mused a little space;

He said, 'She has a lovely face;
God in his mercy lend her grace,
The Lady of Shalott.'

The sense of mystery is preserved in the questions, and the sense of something strange and to be feared in the effects on the palace and the knights. The world of Shalott, the gray world, intrudes into the joyous, active world of Camelot for a moment, and grips it with its stillness. Lancelot alone feels anything but fear for himself; he alone, the unconscious cause of her death, feels pity for her and her beauty, and prays, not for himself, but for her. The power of this conclusion, with its fine irony, is enhanced by the diction, which becomes here extremely simple and direct.

The contrast between the two versions of the poem is not simply that between incompetence and competence. Primarily it is that between an infirm and a firm grasp of the poem's structure. It seems evident that in the 1832 version Tennyson is concentrating on the technical problems posed by the difficult stanza form. As far as a general mode of treatment of the theme is concerned, he seems to see it only as a medieval legend, attractively Romantic in its elements of magic and fairylore, suitable for a rich pictorial development. He accordingly develops it through elaboration of visual description. But at the same time, a sense of the theme central to the 1842 version is in the back of his mind, and appears here and there in the poem. Two things happen in the revision: he gets complete control of the stanza form, so that it no longer dictates to him, no longer forces him into weak padding or into irrelevancies, and he sees very clearly what his poem is about, and how to shape it as a total form.

— F.E.L. Priestly, *Language and Structure in Tennyson's Poetry* (London: Andre Deutsch, 1973): pp. 47–49, 51–52.

HERBERT F. TUCKER ON THE POEM'S FOREIGNNESS

[Herbert F. Tucker is the author of *Browning's Beginnings: The Art of Disclosure* and *Tennyson and the Doom of Romanticism*. In the excerpt below, Tucker discusses the originality of the poem's foreignness.]

Upon Tennyson's removal of *The Lover's Tale* from his 1832 collection, its place at the head of the volume went to a work that is harder, in several senses of that adjective: more tautly assembled, more gnomically difficult, and more pessimistic in its outlook on human relationship and the reciprocation of love. "The Lady of Shalott" so quickly passed through the hands of the foremost Victorian iconographers into the public domain—where it still enjoys a kind of shadow life in the higher pop culture—that its original foreignness may be overlooked, the extent of its alienation underestimated. This is the first of a number of popular Tennyson poems whose very popularity obliges us to estrange ourselves from them if we wish to recover their original force. But here, at least, an intransigent poetic formality makes the work of defamiliarization uncommonly easy to undertake. The division of "The Lady of Shalott" into numbered parts, further subdivided into discrete stanzas, frames it as an art object; and the invincible rhyme scheme of alternating quadruple and triple ply, even when it does not vanquish the poet (as it did in the "waterlily"—"daffodilly"—"water chilly" triplet from stanza 1 in 1832), insists at every turn that we acknowledge its artfulness. This narrative poem, like *The Lover's Tale*, deals principally in description, but its tetrameter lines renounce the freedom of blank-verse pentameter for a line-bound, chastened syntax and a simplified diction, which sacrifice analytic and affective discourse for the different subtlety of symbol. Furthermore, Tennyson entrusts his narrative to an aloof, neutral scribe of outward events who, psychologically speaking, handles the central Lady almost as gingerly as he handles the meteoric Lancelot and the other peripheral figures that step once into the poem and out again. This narrator's very being, the life of his story, seems a function of his indirection; each of the four parts shuts down at the moment when description yields to directly quoted speech.

"The Lady of Shalott" thus presents itself as a Grecian urn in words, a form for contemplation rather than a lesson for understanding. In this sense it gives a little away as do any of Tennyson's earliest poems. Yet it tells the story of a Lady who gives everything away for the sake of contact with someone else—in the very clear Italian of Tennyson's medieval source, *la Damigella di Scalot morì per amore di Lancialotto de Lac*—which is something no major figure in Tennyson even dreamed of doing thus far. The affecting generosity of the protagonist thus seems at odds with the stringency both of the unforgiving plot in which she finds herself and of the rigid verbal structures that convey it. The consistency with which this large-scale imbalance is reinforced through local ambiguities of phrasing suggests that Tennyson was working at cross-purposes on an insoluble conflict: a conflict between his drive toward a new kind of social commitment and his equally strong residual skepticism about the viability of such commitment in an unresponsive world. Seeking to establish the grounds of identity in relationship, where all the major poems of 1832 hope to find them, "The Lady of Shalott" clearly narrates the world's failure to requite the desires of the self. But where the self is constituted in relationship, this can only be half the story: this failure also bespeaks an inner failure to identify the world accurately and embrace its otherness. Far from solving these riddles of identity and identification, the poem devotes itself to setting them forth in ways that suggest their irresolution.

The Lady begins her career in familiar Tennysonian insularity and enclosure, where "the silent isle embowers / The Lady of Shalott" (17–18), and where passive, intransitive, or weakly transitive present-tense verbs collaborate with the rhyme scheme to describe a world of reptetitive sameness: a world that obeys the natural cycle in its symmetries, or that gravitates without urgency downstream to Camelot, where nature and culture gently cohabit. We recognize this world as that of the earlier Tennyson, but part I marks that new direction of his 1832 poems by raising questions about the Lady's identity in relation to the world that surrounds her. When first named in the second stanza, the Lady seems to be precipitated out of her locale and out of a rhyme scheme that imitates its repetitive natural processes: the phrase "The Lady of Shalott" assmues the place taken by "The island of Shalott" in stanza 1, and the genitive preposition suggests that the Lady is but an exhalation or spirit of the place that names her. Stanza 3, however, introduces complicating questions about this apparently straightforward association:

> By the margin, willow-veiled,
> Slide the heavy barges trailed
> By slow horses; and unhailed
> The shallop flitteth silken-sailed
>   Skimming down to Camelot:
> But who hath seen her wave her hand?
> Or at the casement seen her stand?
> Or is she known in all the land,
>   The Lady of Shalott?

— Herbert F. Tucker, *Tennyson and the Doom of Romanticism* (Cambridge, MA: Harvard University Press, 1988): pp. 99–101. ☺

CHRISTOPHER RICKS ON LANCELOT AND DESTRUCTIVE LOVE

[Christopher Ricks is a well-known scholar who has written extensively on the literature of the Romantic and Victorian periods. His critical works include *Keats and Embarassment* and a three-volume edition of *The Poems of Tennyson*. In this excerpt from his biography, *Tennyson,* Ricks emphasizes Lancelot's importance in "The Lady of Shalott" as the one who underscores the theme of destructive love.]

Impatience with "The Lady of Shalott" for being a "tale of magic symbolism" and not that more conclusive thing, an allegory, manifested itself immediately on publication:

The "Lady of Shalott" is a strange ballad, without a perceptible object and as roundabout as

> 'The yellowleavèd waterlily,
> The greensheathèd daffodilly,
> Tremble in the water chilly,
> Round about Shalott.'

We have said that the author shewed no fear of ludicrous associations; but as there is nothing either romantic or pathetic in this piece, he was safe enough with his Shallot, an onion which could make nobody shed tears.

To tears, perhaps not, but people have been moved by the romance and pathos of "The Lady of Shalott." If an allegorical pointer is needed, the best is still that of R. H. Hutton, who said that the poem

> has for its real subject the emptiness of the life of fancy, however rich and brilliant, the utter satiety which compels any true imaginative nature to break through the spell which entrances it in an unreal world or visionary joys. . . . The curse, of course, is that she shall be involved in mortal passions, and suffer the fate of mortals, if she looks away from the shadow to the reality. Nevertheless, the time comes when she braves the curse.

The Lady is not seen, but sometimes heard:

> Only reapers, reaping early
> In among the bearded barley
> Hear a song that echoes cheerly
> From the river winding clearly,

> Down to towered Camelot:
> And by the moon the reaper weary,
> Piling sheaves in uplands airy,
> Listening, whispers, " 'Tis the fairy
> Lady of Shalott."

Each of the four parts ends with something said: the reaper's whisper, the Lady's repining: "I am half sick of shadows," the Lady's cry: "the curse is come upon me," and Lancelot's moment of musing:

> He said, "She has a lovely face;
> God in his mercy lend her grace,
> The Lady of Shalott."

"She knows not what the curse may be"; simply that it forbids her to look directly at life—she must see life only in her mirror. The mirror is not there simply for the fairy tale; it was set behind the tapestry so that the worker could see the effect from the right side. But what brings the Lady to defy the curse?

> And sometimes through the mirror blue
> The knights come riding two and two:
> She hath no loyal knight and true,
> The Lady of Shalott.

Lancelot is not the first knight that she sees, but he rides alone; nor does he have exactly a "loyal" lover; nor is he exactly a "loyal knight and true" (he is "falsely true" to Guinevere and to Arthur). It is the sight of "two young lovers lately wed" which wrings from the lady the cry that mingles weariness and illness: "I am half sick of shadows."

The sight of Lancelot is dazzling:

> All in the blue unclouded weather
> Thick-jewelled shone the saddle-leather,
> The helmet and the helmet-feather
> Burned like one burning flame together,
>   As he rode down to Camelot.

But the sight of Lancelot is piercingly different from any other sight which the Lady sees in the poem. She sees reflected in her mirror both Lancelot and Lancelot reflected in the river:

> From the bank and from the river
> He flashed into the crystal mirror,
> "Tirra lirra," by the river
>   Sang Sir Lancelot.

At which, "She left the web, she left the loom"—and was done for. The "crystal" mirror suggests the river; for the only time in the poem, a word rhymes with itself—a perfect reflection: *river / river.* Nor is there another reference to the river's reflecting in the poem—notably, given that there is so much about the river and about dazzling light. Her mirror constituted a protection against life for the Lady; it cracks after she sees somebody doubly mirrored—"From the bank and from the river"—within the mirror. It is as if the protection is canceled out: re-re-flection = flection, the impact itself.

The Lady slowly dies as by some mysterious suicide, some consumptive wish not to go on living. The river that had been like a mirror is now a "dim expanse"; and the "glassy countenance" is now the Lady's.

Yet the curse seems at once capricious and deeply apt. Tennyson said that "the new-born love for something, for some one in the wide world from which she has been so long secluded, takes her out of the region of shadows into that of realities." She dies in love-birth. But love at such first sight? And are we to think that the reality of love is inherently destructive? Or that it cannot but be destructive once seclusion has long claimed anybody? J. W. Croker, with a wit that is apt as well as hostile, saw the poem basically as a pun on the word *spinster.* But the poem is more of a riddle than that. John Stuart Mill disliked the original 1832 ending, which had quoted the Lady's oracular parchment—"a 'lame and impotent conclusion,' where no conclusion was required." But Tennyson—who was drawn to the right kind of conclusion in which nothing is concluded—did not simply cut out the stanza; he replaced it with Lancelot's musing lines. And in those lines we sense—off the end of the poem again—another destructive love which awaits its catastrophe. When Lancelot says "God in his mercy lend her grace," he speaks as someone to whom God in his mercy will lend grace.

"The Lady of Shalott" is not a perfect poem; it has some Arthurian bric-à-brac and such intentions as the filler "we see" in: "Like to some branch of stars we see / Hung in the golden galaxy." But it creates an intensely memorable myth in which the wish not to face reality and the wish to face it, the impulse toward life and the impulse toward death, an inexplicable guilt and a timorous innocence, shine as from a cracked mirror.

—Christopher Ricks, *Tennyson* (New York: Macmillan, 1972): pp. 79–82. ✍

[Gerhard Joseph is a well-known critic and has written extensively on Tennyson. His critical work includes *Tennyson and the Text: The Weaver's Shuttle* and *Tennysonian Love: The Strange Diagonal*. In the excerpt below, Joseph discusses the importance of the landscape in supplying clues to unanswered questions concerning the Lady's alienation and the curse under which she is forced to live.]

The Lady of Shalott is as alone as both Mariana and Oenone, though in the poem bearing her name the lady has not specifically been deserted. Her isolation receives little narrative elaboration: just as *Measure for Measure* supplies only attenuated hints about the origin of Mariana's predicament, so the reason for the curse upon the Lady of Shalott by which she will die if she tries to enter the real world is unstated. Again one has little more than the landscape of exile: the lady is separated from the world both by water and by height; she is imprisoned on a "silent isle" within "four gray walls, and four gray towers" that "overlook a space of flowers." Tennyson's own description of the poem stresses the lady's epistemological confusion: "The newborn love for something, for someone in the wide world from which she has been so long secluded, takes her out of the region of shadows into that of realities."

But the lady may also illustrate Tennyson's early parabolic treatment of the artist cut off from meaningful contact with the world. In destroying herself as she attempts to enter the world through the "mirror blue," she reflects what Tennyson at this time felt to be the dilemma of the artist. The creation of a sensuous art necessitates the artist's separation from normal activity, especially from the common experience of love:

> But in her web she still delights
> To weave the mirror's magic sights,
> For often thro' the silent nights
> A funeral, with plumes and lights
>   And music, went to Camelot;
> Or when the moon was overhead,
> Came two young lovers lately wed.
>   (ll. 64–70)

The sight of the lovers, framed as in "The Two Voices" and the "Enoch Arden" to come, suddenly makes her "half sick of shadows" and prepares her for the coming of Lancelot. As he moves across her crystal mirror, she hurries to her window to look out upon the rock of reality rather than at its image only. This insistence on a direct encounter with human substance rather than a voyeuristic contemplation of its shadow disintegrates the magic "web with colors gay" and cracks the mirror. Immediately the promised curse descends upon her and precipitates her death, as she floats down the river to Camelot.

Tennyson may thus be dramatizing an opposition that has been emerging throughout his early poetry—an antagonism between art and love that is irresolvable. We have seen that the mermaid and merman affirm the creative role of sense in both art and love—they are at the same time "singers" and "lovers." But the Lady of Shalott finds that the life devoted to the spinning of her magic web of sense is unbearably sterile and that the attempt to loosen the spell and to enter into Hallam's "usual passions of the heart" leads to death. The distance between Hallam's—and Tennyson's—"Sensitive [or Sensuous]" and "Passionate Emotion" looms greater than ever, but now there seems to be no way for the soul of the artist to reconcile the two energies. Tennyson's earlier certainty that the artist must be lord of the five senses and must cultivate his talent secretly within the sacred garden of his mind (see "The Poet's Mind" of 1830) has been undermined, if it has not completely disappeared. The Lady of Shalott is even willing to sacrifice her creative imagination, her mirror and her web, to enter into a human feeling for Lancelot. But she cannot find a meaningful life in either direction; she can neither be satisfied with her magic web nor enter into a circle of ordinary humanity because the "curse" of the artist is upon her. Caught between two worlds to neither of which she can commit herself, she prefigures one of the central themes of the artist in our time.

—Gerhard Joseph, *Tennysonian Love: The Strange Diagonal* (Minneapolis: University of Minnesota Press, 1960): pp. 48–50.

Thematic Analysis of
"Ulysses"

"Ulysses," originally written in 1833 and published in its final form in 1842, is a poem about a familiar epic hero—the Ulysses in Book XI of Homer's *Odyssey* (where Ulysses learns that after killing his wife's suitors he must take a final sea voyage), as well as the Ulysses in Canto XXVI of Dante's *Inferno* (in which he is compelled to give an account of his mysterious journey). Thus, Tennyson's hero reworks a legend taken from both ancient and medieval sources, creating a story of social relevance to the Victorian era, as well as one with personal meaning for Tennyson's own life.

In fact, Tennyson acknowledged a strong autobiographical context for this poem. It was written at the same period in which he was struggling with the loss of Arthur Henry Hallam, and this personal context makes Tennyson's poem a work of mourning for a dearly cherished friend. It also helps to explain its format, which is the dramatic monologue, a genre where the narrator speaks alone, creating a sense of distance between the speaker and his audience, a way of stepping back from a difficult emotional situation. Nevertheless, because an audience or at least an addressee is implied, the speaker is never in complete isolation. However, the audience may be real and external, or wholly internal, existing only in the speaker's mind. In Tennyson's "Ulysses" the hero addresses at least three separate audiences during the course of the poem—but a monologue provides the space for a single voice to represent its own point of view and its own interpretation of the events or story that it narrates.

Ulysses is striving for a way out of a predicament, which is both universally shared among all members of a social body ("It little profits that an idle king . . . met and dole / Unequal laws unto a savage race") and personally relevant (the poet's quest to be reunited with his deceased friend). From the very outset, Ulysses is consumed with an insatiable desire, "a hungry heart," to go beyond the boundaries of human experience and knowledge in order to look into the uncharted territory, "that untravelled world / whose margin fades," of life after death (which, in Dante's story, was an act of great pride, for which any man, hero or otherwise, had to be punished).

In a word, Ulysses is in search of immortality. "To follow knowledge like a sinking star, / Beyond the utmost bound of human thought." That "sinking star" becomes a symbol of the dying hero and points to the underlying theme of his quest—namely, that in longing to be reunited with his friend, Ulysses is expressing a death-wish.

In the first section of the poem (ll. 1–32), Ulysses is speaking to himself, reciting all that is wrong with his homecoming from a prior voyage. He laments the fact that he no longer considers himself a ruler among his people; he has even lost control over his own household, which has been crowded with suitors vying for Penelope's attention (they believed that Ulysses was dead during the long course of his prior journey in the *Odyssey*). These are strangers "[t]hat hoard, and sleep, and feed, and know not me." However, unlike Homer's Ulysses, who is ready to assert his rightful place with his wife and eager to do battle with the trespassers, Tennyson's hero is left with an empty feeling upon his return: "By this still hearth, among these barren crags, / Match'd with an aged wife." Instead, he is anxious to leave as soon as possible, "this gray spirit yearning in desire," on a journey which makes no pretense of return. He wishes to leave this world behind and seek renewal in a life after death. "Life piled on life / Were all too little . . . but every hour is saved / From that eternal silence . . . vile it were / For some three suns to store and hoard myself."

The Lady of Shalott, who longs for the worldly experiences she has been denied, is in sharp contrast with Ulysses, who has been granted the privilege of an extraordinary journey and the fullness of a heroic life, "cities of men / And manners, climates, councils, governments / . . . honor'd of them all—," and yet cannot rest content with all that he has accomplished.

Part II (ll. 33–43) is a direct address by Ulysses to an undefined audience, concerning his son Telemachus, to whom he delegates all authority. "This is my son, mine own Telemachus, / To whom I leave the sceptre and the isle." Here is another contrast, this time between son and father. Telemachus is well balanced and firmly rooted in this world, "[m]ost blameless is he, centred in the sphere," while Ulysses views the piling up of experience as an endless passageway, "an arch wherethro' / Gleams that untravelled world," forever beckoning him to move further on. Furthermore, Telemachus is portrayed as the ideal ruler, cautious in his decisions, one who can be relied upon to treat his subjects fairly, "discerning to fulfil / This labor, by slow prudence" and thereby creating harmony among his people ("thro soft degrees / Subdue them, to the useful and the good"). Ulysses, on the other hand, no longer possesses these leadership qualities. Neither does he hesitate to admit as much to himself and his audience.

His voice imparts a sense of great urgency that each passing moment of delay will only increase the burden of time, where one will "rust unburnish'd, not . . . shine in use!" The reader gets the feeling the sole speaker is about to leave the stage at any given moment, perhaps without finishing his own story.

In Part III (ll. 44–70), Ulysses addresses a third audience, his fellow mariners, and encourages them to make use of their old age. "Free hearts, free foreheads,—you and I are old; / . . . Death closes all; but something ere the end, / Some work of noble note, may yet be done." They are to embark on a journey of no return, a voyage toward death, and that voyage is a frightening exploration of the unknown, where "gloom the dark, broad seas."

Yet despite the foreboding prospects such a journey presents, Ulysses offers two irrefutable arguments to his fellow mariners: First, the voyage to the next world is as unavoidable as the tyrannical and irrepressible power of time. "The long day wanes; the slow moon climbs; the deep / Moans sound with many voices." Second, gesturing toward the next life, though it holds no certainty ("It may be that the gulfs will wash us down; / It may be we shall touch the Happy Isles"), is far more preferable and rewarding than the death-in-life that, from Ulysses' perspective, comes with old age ("Made weak by time and fate / but strong in will / To strive, to seek, to find, and not to yield").

In the end, the advice Ulysses gives to his battle-weary mariners is universal. Lead a purposeful life, he says, while remaining fully aware that time is a precious commodity. The message applies to both the young as well as the old. ❁

Critical Views on
"Ulysses"

WILLIAM WALLACE ROBSON ON TENNYSON'S
AND DANTE'S ULYSSES

[William Wallace Robson has written several books of criticism, which include *Byron as Poet and a Collection of Critical Essays*. In the excerpt below, Robson sees a strong connection between Tennyson's hero and Dante's treatment of Ulysses, while at the same time he recognizes Tennyson's strong social message that one must take responsible public action.]

I begin by quoting one of the most familiar passages of nineteenth-century English poetry.

> The lights begin to twinkle from the rocks:
> The long day wanes: the slow moon climbs: the deep
> Moans round with many voices. Come, my friends,
> 'Tis not too late to seek a newer world.
> Push off, and sitting well in order smite
> The sounding furrows; for my purpose holds
> To sail beyond the sunset, and the baths
> Of all the western stars, until I die.
> It may be that the gulfs will wash us down:
> It may be we shall touch the Happy Isles,
> And see the great Achilles, whom we knew.
> Tho' much is taken, much abides; and tho'
> We are not now that strength which in old days
> Moved earth and heaven; that which we are, we are;
> One equal temper of heroic hearts,
> Made weak by time and fate, but strong in will
> To strive, to seek, to find, and not to yield.

That is the close of Tennyson's 'Ulysses'. It is a very beautiful poem; and I think you will agree that those closing lines derive part of their beauty from a sense we have of a whole history of European imagination and aspiration to which Tennyson is giving voice through the lips of Ulysses. For although he speaks with the accent of Tennyson, the speaker is unmistakably the Ulysses of Dante. In the eleventh book of the *Odyssey* it is foretold that, after his return to Ithaca and the slaying of the suitors, he is to set off again on a mysterious voyage. This voyage, and its sequel, is described by the tragic figure in Dante's *Inferno*. His most famous lines are these, which exhort his companions on his last voyage, beyond the Pillars of Hercules:

> 'O brothers', said I, 'who are come despite
> Ten thousand perils to the West, let none,
> While still our senses hold the vigil slight
> Remaining to us ere our course is run,
> Be willing to forgo experience
> Of the unpeopled world beyond the sun.
> Regard your origin,—from whom and whence!
> Not to exist like brutes, but made were ye
> To follow virtue and intelligence'.

Tennyson's Ulysses is Homer's Odysseus felt through Dante; but the vibration of this poem of Tennyson is not due merely to a modern poet's response to the Renaissance. The emotion to which it gives this dramatic expression is something personal to the poet, as a man alive in his own time. What the poem meant to Tennyson we know. He tells us that 'Ulysses' was written soon after Arthur Hallam's death. 'It gives the feeling [he says] about the need of going forward and braving the struggle of life more simply than anything in "In Memoriam".' As so often in Tennyson, the resolve, the will, to undertake responsible public action and effort, is linked with the need to find release from an overwhelming personal sorrow. This message, then, about 'the need of going forward and braving the struggle of life', is the point of juncture between the poet as a private individual, with his private sorrows, and the poet as a responsible social being, conscious of a public world in which he has duties. The poet in the first place is exhorting himself, to seek consolation in 'going forward'; but he exhorts himself as a responsible social being, and his exhortation—as the tone of the verse so plainly indicates—is equally aimed at a whole moral community of which he is one member.

And it found a response in that community. 'Ulysses' seems to have been what converted Carlyle to a belief in Tennyson. Edward Fitzgerald tells us:

> This was the Poem which, as might perhaps be expected, Carlyle liked best in the Book. [The 1842 volumes.] I do not think he became acquainted with Alfred Tennyson till after these Volumes appeared; being naturally prejudiced against one whom everyone was praising, and praising for a Sort of Poetry he despised. But directly he saw, and heard, the Man, he knew there was A Man to deal with: and took

pains to cultivate him; assiduous in exhorting him to leave Verse and Rhyme, and apply his Genius to Prose and Work.

. . . No one can doubt that admirable Victorian seriousness, which Carlyle saluted in 'Ulysses', is really there; the desire to express it is manifestly an important part of the poem's inspiration. And yet, when we restore that heroic close of the poem to its context—and even when we examine the passage I quoted by itself—there is something to be said about the quality of the verse, the poetic texture, which is strikingly at odds with the judgment—so obviously true— that Tennyson is here at one with an aspiration of his age.

—William Wallace Robson, "The Dilemma of Tennyson," *The Listener* 55 (1957). Reprinted in *Critical Essays on the Poetry of Tennyson*, ed. John Killham (New York: Barnes and Noble Books, 1960): pp. 155–57.

Arthur Ward on Ulysses's Shortsightedness

[In his essay "'Ulysses' and 'Tithonus': Tunnel Vision and Idle Tears," Arthur Ward identifies Ulysses's shortsightedness as the basis for his emotional dilemma. Ulysses, says Ward, is a man trapped in a state of idleness, a hero who needs help defining himself.]

Many readers have noticed that "Ulysses" and "Tithonus" depict similar predicaments. A man who once thought himself almost a god is now old and feeble, trapped in a state of idleness. He yearns toward the West, toward a journey whose last stop will be death. Significantly, in order to escape from his predicament he calls on someone else to help him. Tithonus' monologue is full of pleas that Eos deliver him from his shadow-existence, and Ulysses cannot leave Ithaca without a crew. The last section of "Ulysses," from "There lies the port," is usually read as a piece of rhetoric persuading his mariners to make the voyage.

In both poems, the speaker's call for help reflects ironically upon his moral position and even upon his mental competence. The passivity of Tithonus is not simply a result of old age; it is apparently a lifelong habit. Consider his memory of a long-ago tryst with Eos:

> Ay me! ay me! with what another heart
> In days far-off, and with what other eyes
> I used to watch—if I be he that watched—
> The lucid outline forming round thee; saw
> The dim curls kindle into sunny rings;
> Changed with thy mystic change, and felt my blood
> Glow with the glow that slowly crimsoned all
> Thy presence and thy portals, while I lay,
> Mouth, forehead, eyelids, growing dewy-warm
> With kisses balmier than half-opening buds
> Of April, and could hear the lips that kissed
> Whispering I knew not what of wild and sweet,
> Like that strange song I heard Apollo sing,
> While Ilion like a mist rose into towers.

. . . Ulysses, too, needs help from others in defining himself. He cannot sail off to end his life in some appropriate "work of noble note" without his mariners. Ulysses spends twenty-five lines persuading them to his purpose. Indeed, all the people mentioned in "Ulysses" receive his attention in direct proportion to their importance for his purpose. The mariners are indispensible; hence the twenty-five lines directed at them. Telemachus, who will relieve his father of political responsibilities and thus free him for the voyage, is worth eleven lines of lukewarm praise. Ulysses' subjects are a responsibility just important enough to be onerous; he mentions them twice, two lines each time. Penelope, the finish-line of a race run long ago, is dismissed with two words: "aged wife."

Just as Ulysses' purpose ruthlessly subordinates the people around him, so it subordinates, sometimes distorts, his own past. He summarizes his past in lines seven through seventeen, and the summary is notably vague. Not one of the adventures from the Odyssey is specifically mentioned in these lines, and there is only one reference, a general one, to the Trojan war.

> Much have I seen and known; cities of men
> And manners, climates, councils, governments,
> Myself not least, but honored of them all;
> And drunk delight of battle with my peers,
> Far on the ringing plains of windy Troy.

Ulysses is clearly impatient to finish with the question of his past and go on to a topic he finds much more interesting—his heroic status: "Myself not least, but honored of them all." He insists upon it not out of simple vanity, but in order to justify his purpose. It is natural, he implies, that the peer of the men who fought at Troy cannot rest from travel. It little profits a hero of the old stamp to hoard a few years of tame existence on Ithaca.

John Pettigrew discusses Ulysses' distortions of his past. After asking whether Dante's characterization of Ulisse, once invoked by echoes of the *Inferno*, might be intended to influence our response to Tennyson's Ulysses, Pettigrew concludes,

> No one, of course, would suggest that a new handling of an archetypal figure need necessarily involve assimilating all that figure's characterics, but if no poem has its complete meaning alone, if it is a part of all that it has met in the tradition, an affirmative answer to the question raised above is at least possible.

And if, as I believe, an affirmative answer is not only possible but probable, it applies to echoes of Homer as well as Dante. Christopher Ricks, in his 1969 edition of Tennyson's complete poems, cites three Homeric echoes in "Ulysses": lines 13–14 (*Odyssey* i, 3–5), lines 58–59 (*Odyssey* iv, 580 etc.), and lines 60-61 (*Odyssey* v, 270–275). He further notes that lines 58–59 are direct translations of a Homeric commonplace.

That commonplace, "sitting well in order smite / The sounding furrows," seems designed to evoke for both mariners and readers the memory of *Odyssey* voyages. However, Ulysses addresses his mariners as men "That ever with a frolic welcome took / The thunder and the sunshine, and opposed / Free hearts, free foreheads." If, as Homeric echoes and allusions suggest, what happens in the Odyssey can be considered part of Ulysses' past, then his description of his mariners is grossly inaccurate. They did not take the "thunder"—the terrible storms that drowned so many of them—with anything like "a frolic welcome." Nor is it quite accurate to call Ulysses' past voyages expeditions of "Free hearts, free foreheads." The man who had beaten Thersites for presuming to criticize his betters, and who later drove his grumbling men toward Ithaca with the lash of his will, was not the president of a sea-going republic, but a feudal lord. Either Ulysses is deliberatly glossing over his past to make his pitch to the mariners more persuasive, or something has warped his own memory.

—Arthur Ward, "'Ulysses' and 'Tithonus': Tunnel Vision and Idle Tears," *Victorian Poetry* 12, no. 4 (Winter 1974): pp. 312–14. ☯

E. J. Chiasson on the Poem's Religious Meanings

[In this essay, E. J. Chiasson reads the poem as an expression of Tennyson's belief that religious faith is vital to our well-being. He attempts thus to recuperate a social and spiritual purpose he believes Tennyson to have intended, one that criticism has long overlooked.]

It has long been recognized that Tennyson's *Idylls* are, among other things, the allegorical presentation of ideas which had found their place in a large number of poems, from 'The Palace of Art' to 'Lucretius' and 'The Ancient Sage'. Such fidelity to a set of ideas need not surprise us in a poet who had always felt that 'only under the inspiration of ideals, and with his "sword bathed in heaven", can a man combat the cynical indifference, the intellectual selfishness, the sloth of will, the utilitarian materialism of a transition age.' Yet despite this willingness on the part of critics to arrange much of the Tennyson canon in this perfectly convincing pattern, little attention has been paid to the intractability of 'Ulysses', that is to say, to its virtual refusal to submit to such an arrangement. As a result 'Ulysses' continues to be, what it has always been, something of a 'sport' in Tennyson criticism. Although I do not intend to fit 'Ulysses' into such a pattern by detailed references to the *Idylls,* I shall try to show that critical attention to the poem has stopped short of placing it precisely where it belongs, namely among the many expressions of Tennyson's conviction that religious faith is mandatory for the multitudinous needs of life.

Lacking such a view of the poem, critics of 'Ulysses' (no longer enthusiastically restricting themselves to an admiration of its 'gleam' qualities) think of it generally as a poem of relatively unresolved antimonies. One critic, regarding it as, at least intentionally, a 'gleam' poem, is of course struck by the familiar disturbing Dantean conception of Ulysses's character, and concludes that 'Ulysses' is a brilliant failure in which the 'details are inconsistent, the reasoning specious, the whole a kind of brilliantly whited sepulchre. . . .' Another critic, most perceptive on the whole, sees in the poem evidence of a certain ambivalence in Tennyson's thinking; while still another detects a dichotomy between 'Tennyson's own account of his meaning' and the 'desolate melancholy music of the words themselves. . . .' Charles Tennyson in his recent *Life* returns to the noncommital view that in 'Ulysses' Tennyson 'expressed his realization of the need for going forward and braving the battle of life, in spite of the crushing blow of Arthur's death'.

While it is true that 'Ulysses' was written as a result of Hallam's death, the assumption has too quickly been made that this fact is by itself helpful to an understanding of the poem. The purpose of this essay, therefore, is to suggest as an alternative that in 'Ulysses' Tennyson is elaborating the belief, which was to become perennial with him, that life without faith leads to personal and social dislocation. Briefly stated, the position of this writer is that Tennyson is writing here not a mismanaged 'gleam' poem or a poem which gives evidence of 'the operation of private insights' though 'ostensibly addressed to a Victorian audience,' but a dramatic portrayal of a type of human being who held a set of ideas which Tennyson regarded as destructive of the whole fabric of his society.

It must be confessed that the celebrated passage from Hallam Tennyson's *Memoir* has assisted mightily in reinforcing the view of 'Ulysses' as a paean to heroic effort. For Tennyson is quoted in the *Memoir* as saying: ' "Ulysses" . . . was written soon after Hallam's death, and gave my feeling about the need for going forward, and braving the struggle of life *perhaps more simply than anything in "In Memoriam"*.' Since this statement of purpose is, of course, somewhat cryptic, it is perhaps not surprising that most critics have taken it to mean that the character Ulysses is, in some measure at least, the spokesman of Tennyson, or that it is Ulysses who is to be construed as braving the struggle of life. It is possible, however, to interpret Tennyson's statement of purpose to mean simply that here he has given us his views on the general question of what an adequate pursuit of life means, and has given us no license to assume that Ulysses is his spokesman, or that his architectonics have been obvious. That this wary reading of Tennyson's statement of purpose is not merely wilful is suggested by the italicized part of the above quotation wherein Tennyson asserts that his intention in writing 'Ulysses' was, in some sense at any rate, identical with his intention in writing *In Memoriam*. . . .

In section 34 of *In Memoriam* and elsewhere, Tennyson expresses the pivotal doctrine of his creed, namely that life without immortality is not only meaningless but monstrous. It is indeed the conviction that immortality is a fact which enables him to rise above his despair. Certain corollaries, central to our purpose, follow from this belief. One of them, as we learn from section 35, is that without immortality love would become 'mere fellowship of sluggish moods' or at its coarsest, a bruising and crushing urge which 'bask'd and batten'd in the woods'. Another resultant of this pivotal discovery, as we see from section 66, is a new awareness in the poet of the value of the softer affections, especially within a familial context. Section 106, with its look into the future, is a measure of the more strictly social direction which his exaltation takes after he has conquered his despair. In section 109 he reflects on the great promise that Hallam had given of being 'A potent voice of Parliament A pillar steadfast in the storm.' But especially important to our purpose is Tennyson's statement of dissatisfaction with an extravagant intellectualism divorced from faith and love.

—E. J. Chiasson, "Tennyson's 'Ulysses'—A Re-Interpretation," *University of Toronto Quarterly* 20 (1954). Reprinted in *Critical Essays on the Poetry of Tennyson*, ed. John Killham (New York: Barnes and Noble Books, 1960): pp. 164–66.

Tony Robbins on the Poem's Focus on Mood

[In this essay, Tony Robbins reads the poem as a mood piece that describes the speaker's state of mind—his determination to endure and conquer depression and despair. Unlike other critics, Robbins does not see "Ulysses" as an epic recital of heroic action, as in the *Odyssey*, or as judgment on the legendary hero, as in the *Divine Comedy*.]

The poem's seventy lines are rich in detail, and in quotations and echoes. Yet Tennyson's literary memory, though eclectic, is not haphazard: the reader needs a peculiarly subtle understanding of his poetic method, of the manner in which each detail is used. . . .

In order to appreciate Tennyson's art we need an awareness of the direction and force of each allusion or suggestion, as these arise from the poem's circumstances; the reader's notion of the feeling given in the poem will be informed as much by his head as by his sensibility.

Browning's preoccupation is generally with historical figures, or with figures imaginable in a precise historical context. Tennyson's, by contrast, is with legendary figures. (One writes *The Ring and the Book*; the other, *Idylls of the King*.) Tennyson deliberately chose imperfectly treated classical subjects so that he "might have free scope for his imagination." In the case of "Ulysses," neither Tiresias' prophecy of Odysseus' manner of dying, in *Odyssey* XI, nor the relation of Ulisse in Dante's *Inferno* xxvi, is full or detailed. Tennyson has used both with considerable discrimination. As I shall show, in doing so he concentrates on the lyrical element of his poem, on its possibilities for the communication of a predominant feeling, and precludes the kind of judgment on his central figure implicit in the dramatic monologue. . . . The mood itself at once contains and is expressed by the poem's cumulative detail, which suggests a complex of thoughts and feelings about the speaker's situation. "Ulysses" is, in part, a poem of literary experience (if I may so adapt Robert Langbaum's phrase): the "object" of the poet's mind's eye is a literary character, as known in Homer's epics and Dante's *Commedia*. Tennyson's own experience of the two figures Odysseus and Ulisse becomes in this poem his experience of a third, his own Ulysses, whose speech holds "in a medium of strong emotion" the circumstances and details most appropriate to the mood of the new literary figure and that of the poet himself. They are, finally, one and the same, and the unusual proof of this lies in the Eversley note, which relates the mood of "Ulysses" to the time soon after Hallam's death.

For these reasons, characterization, setting, and the emphasis of a particular point of view are not strong elements in the poem. Its purpose is not so much to portray a particular individual by juxtaposing distinct details of speech and scene, as to suggest a particular mood, or, to use Eliot's phrase, a structural emotion. It is for the sake of this feeling that the literary experience of Homer and Dante is invoked, and it is to this end that the details of that experience are chosen and ordered within the poem.

The obvious general allusion to Odysseus . . . reminds us of the attraction of the simple heroic refusal to die. It is this spirit that Ulysses, descendant of the literary figure who roused the lotos-eaters and drove them to their ships, seeks to call up in himself and his mariners. At the same time, implicit in the poem is the *need* for vigor. In the fourth paragraph, Tennyson adopts the habitual time of day for setting out on a voyage, evening, but associates it with the ending of life as well as of the day, with the decline of manly strength as well as that of the sun:

> There lies the port; the vessel puffs her sail:
> There gloom the dark broad seas. My mariners,

Souls that have toiled, and wrought, and thought with me—
That ever with a frolic welcome took
The thunder and the sunshine, and opposed
Free hearts, free foreheads—you and I are old;
Old age hath yet his honour and his toil;
Death closes all: but something ere the end,
Some work of noble note may yet be done,
Not unbecoming men that strove with Gods.
The lights begin to twinkle from the rocks:
The long day wanes: the slow moon climbs: the deep
Moans round with many voices. Come, my friends,
'Tis not too late to seek a newer world.

. . . Tennyson's poem relates no action, yet it develops an evocation of the frame of mind in which action might be undertaken. This is evoked cumulatively by an alternation of tone and movement as of thought. In the first and third paragraphs (ll. 1–5, 33–43), Ulysses speaks, first harshly, then mildly, of the world he would leave behind and of his son's role there. In the longer second and fourth paragraphs (ll. 6–32, 44–70), he looks outwards. Within each of these longer paragraphs the cadences swell and fall with the alternation of the feelings expressed. The second paragraph has two principal themes: one, taken up with his memories and his fame, shifts into a generalized expression of his timeless nature (ll. 6–21); the other, concerned with his conception of the manner in which life should be lived, leads to another view of himself "yearning" to set off in pursuit of "knowledge" (ll. 22–32). In both sections of the paragraph, the movement of the verse slows perceptibly towards the close. In the fourth paragraph the opening evocation of evening is followed by an energetic recollection of past achievement, then by a somber statement of the possibilities of old age, leading to the second evocation of evening—itself succeeded by some vigorous phrases, which modulate into a second momentary awareness of death. That final nine lines of the poem (ll. 62ff), displaying a weighty use of parallelism and repetition, are level and solid, as the resolution of these alternating moods is reached. Ulysses reproduces in the structure of his speech his own mental act in deciding to leave Ithaca and attempt "some work of noble note," miming within the fourth paragraph the act of rousing himself and others from the lethargy of old age.

—Tony Robbins, "Tennyson's 'Ulysses': The Significance of the Homeric and Dantesque Backgrounds," *Victorian Poetry* 11, no. 3 (Autumn 1973): pp. 277–81. ℗

Thematic Analysis of
Locksley Hall

Locksley Hall, originally written in 1835 and published in final form in 1842, is a complex poem encompassing many of the personal issues and social concerns with which Tennyson grappled throughout his life and work. The poem begins as an adolescent crisis poem in which the youthful speaker laments, among other things, the loss of his beloved cousin Amy ("her eyes on all my motions with a mute observance hung") and, as many critics have pointed out, a loss of faith in his own poetic abilities as a result of being estranged from the object of his desire ("O the dreary, dreary moorland! O the barren, barren shore"). The poem ends with a successful resolution of these psychological problems through a renewed self-confidence, especially in his own poetic talents ("So I triumphed ere my passion sweeping thro' me left me dry"), and a belief in social progress and the promise of future. This promise is made all the more confident when we observe the poet turn a prior melancholic statement of hopelessness "when he dipt into the future" (ll. 15 and 16) into an unwavering, absolute declaration that the best is yet to come, a joyous anticipation of endless possibilities. "For I dipt into the future, far as human eye could see / Saw the Vision of the world, and all the wonder that would be" (ll. 119-20). The youthful speaker works through his personal sense of anxiety and hopelessness by reading the spiritual message contained in Nature, and through this meditation, leaves the fictitious world of Locksley Hall in both full possession and joyous expectation of his creative abilities.

Locksley Hall is a poem replete with an enormous energy exerted by its plaintive voice. Its successful transformation of new and disturbing experiences occurs, as always with Tennyson, through the medium of language. Language provides the means to constantly reinvent ways to explain to ourselves what would otherwise be overwhelming pain. Language transforms doubt and despair ("[w]hen I clung to all the present for the promise that it closed") into a vision of infinite possibilities ("O, I see the crescent promise of my spirit hath not set, / Ancient founds of inspiration well thro' all my fancy set").

Locksley Hall is set in the form of a dramatic monologue, which, as in "Ulysses," creates a sense of distance between the speaker and his audience, providing a way of stepping back from a difficult emotional situation. However, unlike the free verse form of "Ulysses," this poem is written in a trochaic rhyme scheme, a trochee being a metrical foot in which a long syllable is followed by a short syllable. According to J. Hagen in her article "The 'Crescent Promise' of 'Locksley Hall': A Crisis in Poetic Creativity," this rhyme scheme creates a "rocking horse rhythm."

A rocking horse is an apt metaphor for a poem in which the speaking voice conveys the experience of working through his many mood swings. In the opening lines the young man wavers between a melancholic inertia caused by the "[d]reary gleams about the moorland flying" and the possibility of future action. "Comrades, leave me here a little, while as yet 't is early morn; / Leave me here, and when you want me, sound upon the bugle-horn."

Locksley Hall, as mentioned above, is also a fictitious realm, although geographically placed somewhere along the coast of Lincolnshire, and the occasion, namely Amy's rejection of the young man at her domineering father's insistence, a "[p]uppet to a father's threat," is equally fictitious. However, *Locksley Hall* does have some veiled autobiographical references, either to Tennyson's brother Frederick, whose infatuation with his cousin Julia was also thwarted by her parents, or possibly to the poet's love for Rosa Barring, to whom he had written love poems between 1834 and 1836 and from whom he too was separated through parental intervention. Thus, parental insensitivity toward true love, the imposition of parents' own narrow concerns that do not allow for a consideration of the lovers' plight, is the initiating event of this poem.

This crisis is first expressed through the creation of a moody landscape, a bleak terrain in which Nature is made to reflect the young man's anguish, a place where he can indulge his depressed state of mind, "nourishing a youth sublime." Indeed, this is a place where Nature is out of synch with "universal law" and the cyclical changes of the seasons. Here it no longer promises the renewal of spring, when "a young man's fancy lightly turns to thoughts of love," but instead conforms to the young man's bleak perspective on the loss of his beloved Amy.

Further, the astronomical references to the "great Orion sloping slowly to the west" and the "Pleiads, rising thro' the mellow shade" serve two purposes here. First, these are constellations that are especially brilliant in winter and spring—but in *Locksley Hall* they are enervated symbols of a dreary landscape that can only mirror the speaker's depressed feelings.

In a brief note on *Locksley Hall* Traci Gardner discusses the mythological significance of the Orion allusion. Orion, a figure in Roman mythology, fell in love with Merope and hoped to marry her, only to be thwarted by Merope's father, Oenopian, the King of Chios. When the desperate Orion attempted to defy the King, he was blinded and cast out onto the beach. The story obviously parallels the themes of *Locksley Hall.*

Finally, the poem contains images of the cruelties of time, its preternatural speed, "[e]very moment, lightly shaken ran itself in golden sands," and its ravage of both the lovers' relationship and the speaker's creative abilities. "Love took up the harp of Life, and smote on all the chords with might" and in so doing destroyed the harmony symbolized by the harp. Instead, love becomes an adversary, destroying the loveliness of the harp with a tyrannical force. When he expresses the tyranny of love and time, Tennyson's choice of the word "smote" is significant. Taken from the Old English verb "smiten," the image here has two important applications: it describes, simultaneously, both the act of using a weapon to inflict serious injury or death and the act of touching a harp so as to produce musical sounds. Furthermore, the idea of the musical sounds of a harp being dealt a mighty and violent blow are akin to the speaker's feeling a loss of poetic power.

Having painted a sympathetic background to his feelings, the speaker turns again to address Amy, "O my Amy, mine no more!" and offers his prognostications as to what her fate will be with an inferior lover whom her father finds acceptable. "Yet it shall be; thou shalt lower to his level day by day, / what is fine within thee growing coarse to sympathize with clay." The forsaken lover thus predicts that Amy will have no other choice but to bow to the desires of a very undesirable husband. "As the husband is, the wife is; thou art mated with a clown, / And the grossness of his nature will have weight to drag thee down." Here, the word *clown* is used in its original meaning, that of a peasant or rustic, usually implying someone who is ignorant and crass in manners.

At this point in the poem, the only antidote to this insufferable situation, the only way out, is in the speaker's imagining a quasi-suicidal resolution. "Better thou and I were lying, hidden from the heart's disgrace, / Roll'd in one another's arms, and silent in a last embrace." Indeed, these lines can be understood as an allusion to John Keats, a Romantic poet who greatly influenced Tennyson. In Keats's poem, "Ode on a Grecian Urn," the lovers represented on the urn are in a state of arrested animation, and because they are unable to act upon their feelings, they have the ability to hold on to their hope forever. "Bold lover, never, never canst thou kiss, / Though winning near the goal—yet do not grieve: / She cannot fade, though thou hast not thy bliss, / For ever wilt thou love, and she be fair." Though Keats's lovers are far beyond the grip of time and human interference, we are made to feel that any attempt to consummate their love will prove to be immediately fatal. In a word, their love is absolutely impossible. We hear these same echoes in *Locksley Hall.*

Having proclaimed his love for Amy as impossible, the speaker now turns to the social injustices that impinge on their relationship. In doing so, he introduces another opposition where culture becomes an adversary of nature, an issue that consumed both Romantic and Victorian writers alike. "Cursed be the social wants that sin against the strength of youth! / Cursed be the social lies that warp us from the living truth?" That social relevance is even made to include the disenfranchised workers whose rights at that time were being asserted by the Chartists, champions of the discontented masses, "a hungry people, as a lion, creeping nigher." These grievances that need to be redressed are combined with the personal relationship that was truncated and forbidden before it had a chance to live.

The rejected lover now speaks his truth in maxims, brief but pithy pronouncements on the harm that can be caused when unsympathetic parents (or political figures in the larger sense) give in to selfish interests. "O, the child too clothes the father with a dearness not his due. / Half is thine and half is his; it will be worthy of the two." This pronouncement likewise alludes to another one of Tennyson's Romantic forebears, William Wordsworth, and the epigram to his "Ode on Intimations of Immortality." "The child is father to the man / And I could wish my days to be / Bound each to each by natural piety."

In Tennyson's allusion to Wordsworth we may read a turning point in *Locksley Hall,* a point at which the speaker's vision of the future is reopened, where "[e]very door is barr'd with gold, and opens but to golden keys," and where he is finally released from melancholic inertia. "Overlive it—lower yet—be happy! Wherefore should I care? /I myself must mix with action, lest I wither by despair." From this point forward, the speaker is reanimated with a tremendous energy, ready to offer an exuberant response to life, and in that response is the hope and promise of a return to his former poetic abilities. He prays to Nature, his inspiring Muse, "O thou wondrous Mother-Age! / Make me feel the wild pulsation that I felt before the strife, when I heard my days before me, and the tumult of my life."

Locksley Hall ends with the speaker feeling all the strength of youth, creating a race of "iron-jointed, supple-sinew'd" young warriors, who will look to Nature for the inspiration to strive for whatever goals they choose and find there a consoling sympathy when those goals seem merely a dream. "They shall dive, and they shall run, / Catch the wild goat by the hair . . . / Whistle back the parrot's call and leap the rainbows of the brooks / Not with blinded eyesight poring over miserable books." And, with this declaration of success in the renewal brought by Nature, the young man leaves Locksley Hall, "[l]et it fall . . . with rain or hail, or fire or snow." However, his vow to no longer pore "over miserable books" rings ironic, for he has made abundantly clear that other poets have taught him how to "read" nature; books, thus, are the true source of his inspiration. ❦

Critical Views on
Locksley Hall

CLYDE DE L. RYALS ON THE NARRATIVE FORM
OF THE MONOLOGUE

[Clyde de L. Ryals is the author of several books on the Victorian and Romantic period, including *A World of Possibilities: Romantic Irony in Victorian Literature*, and *Theme and Symbol in Tennyson's Poems to 1850*, from which this extract was taken. Ryals discusses how the narrative form of the monologue in *Locksley Hall* is a device that enables the young man to distance himself from personal and social issues, thereby allowing him to achieve a resolution to those problems.]

"Locksley Hall" . . . presents us with another Byronic hero who suffers all the disaffection of earlier Tennysonian protagonists but who in the end yields his sense of alienation to a belief in progress. The poem is, thus, closely allied to "The Two Voices" since there are two conflicting forces—voices of despair and comfort—contending for his soul; and in form the poem is an interplay of opposites: love and hate, regression and aggression, isolation and social involvement, present misery and future progress. Yet "Locksley Hall" is less personal than "The Two Voices," for by means of the monologue employing a *persona* Tennyson is in part objectifying his own situation, seeing his problems through the eyes of someone else. Resorting to a poem relating an experience, he hoped to find vicarious meaning for himself. Furthermore, the mask served as a safety device: the hero could be repudiated if necessary. In fact, Tennyson felt it incumbent upon him to separate the speaker in "Locksley Hall" from himself, for he insisted that "the hero is imaginary," that the poem was merely a representation of "young life, its good side, its deficiencies, and its yearnings." By this remark one is reminded of Browning's disclaimer attached to his 1842 *Dramatic Lyrics* that his monologues were "so many utterances of so many imaginary persons, not mine." In spite of Tennyson's statement, however, we can see fairly clearly through the disguise that the speaker does represent many of the attitudes examined in other Tennyson poems.

The monologue opens with the speaker, like other disaffected Tennyson heroes an orphan, viewing the Hall, and almost immediately he assumes the dark mask of age, reverting to a happier past when the world offered promises of fruitfulness. In the present, however, "all things here are out of joint," "the individual withers, and the world is more and more"; and Amy's loveless marriage is but symptomatic of the decadent moral state of a commercial society. Better were it to die, to be "Roll'd in one another's arms, and silent in a last embrace," and so to escape by death "the social lies that warp us from the living truth!" But the death wish is fleeting, and the speaker resorts to memory as an escape, which also proves unsatisfying. In a regressive moment he begs, "Hide me from my deep emotion, O thou wondrous Mother Age," at the same time realizing that "I myself must mix with action, lest I wither by despair." In spite of the visions of humanitarian progress, he is not able to shake loose from his despair, and he considers escaping to the Orient and becoming a Byronic wanderer. . . .

At the close of the poem the speaker finds resolution when he, "the heir of all the ages," realizes that the past has made the present and that the past and present together will join to make "the great world spin for ever down the ringing grooves of change." He has been able to find again the inspiration he enjoyed as a child. He can bid farewell to Locksley Hall, for he has ridded himself of his obsessive concern with the Hall as a symbol of despair.

—Clyde de L. Ryals, *Theme and Symbol in Tennyson's Poems to 1850* (Philadelphia: University of Pennsylvania Press, 1964): pp. 123–25.

ROBERT CUMMINGS ON THE MEANING OF THE POEM'S METER

[Robert Cummings is the editor of *Spenser: The Critical Heritage*. In the excerpt below, he discusses the meaning implied by Tennyson's choice of meter in the poem.]

Comrades, leave me here a little, while as yet 'tis early morn;
Leave me here, and when you want me, sound upon the
bugle horn.

'Mr [Henry] Hallam said to me that the English people liked verse in trochaics, so I wrote the poem in this metre.' Perhaps English people like trochaics, but the decision, rather defensively described here, is now usually reckoned unfortunate. The fault is not so much with the trochaics as with the length of the line: eight stresses are too many. Ruskin argues that even trochaic pentameter is 'helplessly prosaic and unreadable'; and while it is clearly not the case that *Locksley Hall* is metrically incoherent in this way, its coherence is bought at a price. Read with the rhythm emphatically marked, the line splits into two manageable halves of four stresses each. These primitive 'gutsy heroics' have always been open to parody. If the strictly trochaic pattern is allowed to dominate in Tennyson's poem, the tripping rhythm accentuates what is most banal in the sentiment. Hopkins's friend Dixon complains that the metre 'had the effect of being artificial and light: most unfit for intense passion'. The customary reading may, however, be wrongly based. Hallam Tennyson quotes from Emerson the opinion that '*Locksley Hall* and *The Two Voices* are meditative poems, which were slowly written to be read slowly'; and indeed, when Henry James heard Tennyson read *Locksley Hall*, he talked of its 'organ roll', its 'monotonous majesty', its 'long echo', but of its being, as it were, drained of everything he might have expected of it. And the likely consequence of mitigating the insistence of the trochees is that the rhythm collapses altogether into something close to prose. Pleading for a slow reading Dwight Culler complains that 'we do not know how to read trochaics any more'. In effect, no one knows how the line should be read. No one knows with what recognizable metre 'this figment of trochaic tetrameter' can profitably be identified.

Tennyson attempts in this poem to write *long* lines in a rhythmically coherent fashion. Whether or not his intentions are fulfilled, it may be helpful to know what they might have been. Long lines may be improvised by adapting or compoundign more familiar metrical schemes. Tennyson's long line would on this principle be cobbled together out of two shorter four-stress ones. The substitution of trochaic feet for iambic ones, despite the superior rapidity which follows, cannot of itself check this form of the line's reversion to its components. In isolation the line may appear unscannable: the fragile iambic fourteeners of *The Flight* (written about the same time as *Locksley Hall*) are momentarily relieved by a trochaic fifteener that in its context looks almost prosy:

> Than to waken every morning to that face I loathe to see.

But that is not a line manufactured out of two short ones. Some fifteener lines are. The trochaic fifteeners of W. E. Ayton's version of Homer, published before *Locksley Hall* and which have been adduced as Tennyson's precedent, are certainly of this kind, identical with the trochaic ballad metre which Ayton elsewhere employs. Even if this were truly a precedent, it would be precisely the one not wanted, the one that authorizes the unfortunate tendency of the line to revert to jig. It is already a powerful tendency. Any accumulation of trochaic fifteeners will push into prominence the pattern dominant in English verse—four stresses distributed along each of four lines. That is, readers instinctively reach for the common denominator of the whole sequence, and they fall back on what they know—a pattern familiar, perhaps insistently so, from hymnody: 'Hush my Dear, lie still and slumber, / Holy Angels guard thy Bed!'. Only a very firm counter-authority for the rhythm will prevent resort to it. But no precedent has been adduced that would authorize the probability of a long line constructed otherwise than on a principle of improvisation. Tennyson's success with *Locksley Hall* is by no means indisputable. But surely something other than the formal arrangement of rhymes distinguishes the metre of *Locksley Hall* from that of *The Lord of Burleigh,* with which Pyre compares it, but which Tennyson himself was concerned might be 'too familiar for public taste'.

—Robert Cummings, "Tennyson, Trench, Tholuck and the 'Oriental' Metre of *Locksley Hall." Translation and Literature* (1992): pp. 127–28.

June Steffensen Hagen on the Poetic Personality of the Speaker

> [June Steffensen Hagen is the author of *Tennyson and His Publishers*. In the excerpt below, Hagen emphasizes the poetic personality of the speaker and finds the poem highly effective in that it forces us to understand the young man's feelings.]

I suggest that the psychological realism and a poetic crisis theme make Tennyson's narrative of the young poet faced by frustrated love and loss of creative power an effective poem.

"Locksley Hall" has dramatic force because of the personality of its speaker; the poem is primarily the self-revelation of a character who is inconsistent in personality, who displays youthful, flighty human nature in all its late adolescent flamboyance and confusion. Tennyson's method is to mix humor, satire, and irony with psychological realism. The important article by R. B. Hovey delineates Tennyson's interest in the "non-rational motivations of human behavior" and the "psychiatric and moral truism that love frustrated breeds hate." Hovey notes that the poem has the "logic of feelings" rather than the logic of one mood. "The poem defines the vagaries of the mood of frustrated love, tracing them naturalistically, convincingly." The hero's neurosis takes variously the forms of narcissism, masochism, sadism, and regression. And like the movement of "Prufrock," the connections in "Locksley Hall" are either half-conscious or unconscious. . . .

The real crisis in the poem is not that of love—that crisis had already passed; the fundamental crisis is one of poetic creativity. The speaker feels that his ability to write poetry has departed along with his love. Now he is asking himself: "What should be my objective in life, my occupation, now that my poetic abilities have gone?" The resolution of this identity quest comes with lines 185–188:

> Mother-Age (for mine I know not) help me as when life begun:
> Rift the hills, and roll the waters, flash the lightnings, weigh the Sun—
>
> O, I see the crescent promise of my spirit hath not set.
> Ancient founts of inspiration well through all my fancy yet.

In line 186 he learns, from his own poetic virtuosity, that he can still write poetry, that he retains ancient inspiration, myth, and even model—and the two lines following are his expression of that new knowledge; his "crescent promise" is still shining. References to his initiation into poetry come in earlier lines: "Love took up the harp of Life, and smote on all the chords with might; / Smote the chord of Self, that, trembling, passed in music out of sight" (ll. 33–34). The speaker's anxiety is understandable: if love made him a poet originally, the removal of love will take away his ability. In line 102 ("I have an angry fancy: what is that which I should do?"), his creative power of imagination (his "fancy") has been defeated by his anger. He faces the identity question openly for the first time.

Dream and fantasy and dramatic recollection are present in this identity quest. The time sequence confuses because experiences are being reviewed as though they were happening in the present; the poem is both "emotion recollected" (but not "in tranquility") and a series of emotional situations felt fresh for the first time. Several levels of memory, too, participate. For example, the speaker goes through a personal infancy regression, beginning with lines 153–154, "Ah, for some retreat / Deep in yonder shining Orient, where my life began to beat," but he also connects this desire with a regression into the infancy of the world itself. Thus, lines 157–172, in which the speaker yearns "to burst all links of habit" by wandering on the islands "at the gateways of the day" where "methinks would be enjoyment more than in this march of mind, / In the steamship, in the railway, in the thoughts that shake mankind," are not *Tennyson's* desires at all, as they are frequently misread. And the forceful, "I will take some savage woman, she shall rear my dusky race," which essentially concludes the world-infancy fantasy, is simply a stage in the disillusioned speaker-poet's movement from the personal to the mythic level of memory....

Near the end, the speaker switches back again to the present with this first line, a key one for reading the whole poem: "Fool, again the dream, the fancy! but I *know* my words are wild" (l. 173). The italics indicate Tennyson's emphasis on the speaker's growing awareness of himself. Increased self-confidence, especially about his own poetic powers, spurs the speaker on to say his "long farewell to Locksley Hall."

—June Steffensen Hagen, "The 'Crescent Promise' of 'Locksley Hall': A Crisis in Poetic Creativity," *Victorian Poetry* 11, no. 2 (Summer 1973): pp. 169–71.

TRACI GARDNER ON THE MYTH OF ORION IN THE POEM

[In this article, Traci Gardner discusses the myth of Orion and Merope as it relates to the young man's predicament in the poem.]

In the opening lines of Tennyson's "Locksley Hall," the speaker remembers evenings when he observed the constellation Orion. Yet, Tennyson expects his reader to see more than this seemingly casual observation. Tennyson has specifically chosen the constellation Orion because the mythological and astronomical situation of the classical Roman character mirrors the present condition of the speaker.

The speaker's failed engagement to Amy is defined by its parallel to Orion's relationship to Merope. Orion fell in love with Merope and wanted to marry her, but her father, Oenopian, the King of Chios, refused to consent to the marriage. Because of Orion's violent attempt to take Merope, he was blinded and cast out onto the beach. The speaker suggests that his marriage was similarly denied—Amy was "puppet to a father's threat, and servile to a shrewish tongue" (l. 42). While the speaker does not admit committing any violent act to gain Amy's hand in marriage, he does have a "jaundiced eye; / Eye to which all order festers, all things are out of joint" (ll. 132–33). The speaker no longer views things as he did prior to Amy's rejection; he has been blinded by her refusal.

Further, much as Orion thought of his lost Merope, the speaker contemplates his loss of Amy as he wanders the beach of Locksley Hall in the opening of the poem. The speaker continues to walk the "moorland" until he is called by his "merry comrades... sounding on the bugle-horn" (l. 145). Thus, the speaker is called to join the hunters just as Orion was called to join the huntress Diana. Appropriately, the speaker's present attitude toward marriage would qualify him to be one of Diana's band as she is also the virgin goddess. Both the mythological Orion and the speaker, then, are rejected by love, blinded, and cast out to hunt for happiness.

Tennyson underscores the differences between the speaker and Amy's husband by comparing Orion's astronomical relationship to Sirius to the speaker's relationship with Amy's husband. In his analysis of the parallels between the speaker and Orion, E. C. Bufkin noted that Amy's husband offers a contrast to the speaker since the husband is merely a man who "hunts in dreams," and the speaker, like Orion, is a true hunter. Though Bufkin asserts that "the ironical contrast between the giant Orion and the man of small worth is effective as it is subtle," the contrast is even more effective when the subtle importance of Orion's position in the sky is compared to Tennyson's full line. . . .

Tennyson's allusion to these mythological and astronomical parallels heighten the speaker's agony and pain. The speaker is not a mere man rejected by love—he is a mythic giant refused by his beloved princess; the speaker's situation grows from a gentleman's misfortune to a mythic hero's lost love.

—Traci Gardner, "Tennyson's 'Locksley Hall,'" *Explicator* 44, no. 2 (Winter 1986): pp. 23–25.

Thematic Analysis of
"Tears, Idle Tears"

Published in 1847, "Tears, Idle Tears" is a poem within a larger group of poems entitled *The Princess*. In general terms, the agenda for *The Princess* was to discuss the relations between the sexes in contemporary culture and to argue for women's rights, specifically in higher education. But for all this, in presenting a variety of perspectives *The Princess* also avoids taking responsibility for any single point of view. Thus, it may be seen as providing us with a series of cues and directions as to how people interact socially and how the individual soul makes its way in the world.

In the end, what *The Princess* accomplishes is what can be said of all of Tennyson's work: namely, it avoids telling a coherent story, and it is difficult to pin down in terms of theme; in fact, as with so many of Tennyson's poems, the reader cannot reach any definite conclusion by the end of the poem. What Tennyson does successfully accomplish is the evocation of an emotional state, expressing complex feelings on the part of his speakers through the use of strong imagery.

Therefore, when we come to discuss a much smaller, isolated instance within that larger group of poems, such as "Tears, Idle Tears," we are at least prepared for an interpretive experience that will yield no easy answers. Indeed, of all the poems discussed in this book, "Tears, Idle Tears" is by far the shortest and yet most enigmatic; indeed, it lacks any plot or clear position in time or place from which we can begin. Nonetheless, despite the absence of a clear-cut story or easily recognizable theme, this poem is a brilliant summation about poetic thinking and is very much a product of the times in which Tennyson lived. It also expresses the way in which time itself was understood.

This last aspect, time—or temporality—and the ability of language to impose order, understanding, and clarity on the human condition, has a very long literary history. For Tennyson, the passage of time did not necessarily mean that one progressed toward a definite goal or that time even produced movement. J. Hillis Miller, in his article "Temporal Topographies: Tennyson's Tears," has said that this is a poem about "poetic thinking" on nature, time, and the use of spatial images to adequately express our experience of time, life, and death (or the promise of reward and happiness in a life after death). "Since we lack adequate specifically temporal language, we Westerners always express time (and falsify it) in some spatial image or other, for example in the movement of the hands of a clock."

Thus, what follows is a discussion of the imagery in each of the four stanzas and the questions Tennyson raises and possibly answers in this very short yet complex poem.

The very first line of the first stanza presents us with the fundamental paradox of the entire poem: how can tears, a bodily response to an emotional situation, a type of silent language charged with an abundance of unarticulated feelings, be described as "idle," a word that denotes a lack of direction or purpose, a lack of worth or value, a predisposition to be lazy and, even in a mechanistic sense, a wasted expenditure of energy, as when a machine moves while standing in place? The situation is further distressing because the speaker does not even know the tears' source ("I know not what they mean"), yet their very production requires an enormous expenditure of cooperative energy from the heart and the eyes, which are the gateway to the soul.

Tears are an involuntary response, yet they are visible signs of acute emotional affliction; therefore they can reveal secret feelings we would otherwise never disclose to another living being. Thus, the poem implies the violation of a secret and the inability to stay the consequences, since the source of this outpouring of emotion is a complete mystery.

The speaker's dilemma is made all the more profound in the next line, when we are told that the tears emanate "from the depth of some divine despair," for here the cause is attributed to a type of god who no longer possesses the ability to change the world. Even the use of the phrase "some divine" indicates a feeling of spiritual loss and separation, a guiding principle now gone and departed. The speaking voice is devoid of faith, and this crisis precipitates a complete loss of hope for future happiness. Progress, movement, or useful purpose is no longer possible.

In the second stanza, the image of time is rendered in terms of the speaker sailing on a cruel ocean, which brings back short-lived visions of beloved friends from a suggested mythical underworld, only to return those same beloved friends to the depths from whence they came. "Fresh as the first beam glittering on a sail, / That brings our friends up from the underworld." That reunion is itself a cruel trick of time, as brief as the setting sun, "[s]ad as the last which reddens over one," the outcome of which leads to another form of a lost perspective, a vanishing horizon and the lack of hope for any future visitation with loved ones. The soul plunges into the extreme edge of abject melancholy, "[t]hat sinks with all we love below the verge."

In the third stanza, Nature itself seems to be the victim of the vagaries of time out of joint, as we are given a description of a dark and foreboding summer landscape, where the sun has departed and the song falls on deaf ears. "Ah, sad and strange as in dark summer dawns / The earliest pipe of half-awaken'd birds / To dying ears." Nature is now in a strangely similar predicament with the speaker, whereby Nature too has lost all hope of the regeneration that normally comes with the continual death and rebirth of the seasons.

And yet Nature is not living in a sympathetic relationship to the aggrieved speaker. Rather, the temporality of this third stanza could be described as "parallel time," with Nature miming the speaker's emotional state while wholly disconnected from him. The stanza ends with the speaker dying in some unspecified way as "[t]he casement slowly grows a glimmering square," yet another image of time closing in, like a shrinking picture frame, the vanishing horizon, and the loss of hopeful expectation.

The fourth and last stanza is the most poignant of all, the painful memory of "remember'd kisses after death / And sweet as those by hopeless fancy feign'd," where time is a place, an "invisible medium." Time becomes an imaginary space where we can indulge our bittersweet memories of those we have lost and even imagine their return. But time exerts a tyranny that none can escape and in this last stanza is Tennyson's conscious and deliberate acknowledgment that time is a necessary fiction, a story we must invent through the medium of language, in order to come to terms with that which is otherwise invisible and unfathomable. But that inability to reverse the tyranny of time and hold it captive to our own wishes is a "Death in Life, the days that are no more." ❧

Critical Views on
"Tears, Idle Tears"

CLEANTH BROOKS ON THE MOTIVATIONS
OF THE POEM'S SPEAKER

[Cleanth Brooks is a well-known and highly respected literary critic. His critical works include *William Faulkner: Toward Yoknapatawpha and Beyond* (1978) and *The Well-Wrought Urn: Studies in the Structure of Poetry* (1947). In the excerpt below, Brooks discusses some of the complexities involved for the reader in deciding whether or not the speaker's tears are idle.]

Any account of the poem may very well begin with a consideration of the nature of the tears. Are they *idle* tears? Or are they not rather the most meaningful of tears? Does not the very fact that they are 'idle' (that is, tears occasioned by no immediate grief) become in itself a guarantee of the fact that they spring from a deeper, more universal cause? . . .

The tears 'rise in the heart' as the speaker looks upon a scene of beauty and tranquility. Does looking on the 'happy Autumn-fields' bring to mind the days that are no more? The poet does not say so. The tears rise to the eyes in looking on the 'happy Autumn-fields' *and* thinking of the days that are no more. The poet himself does not stand responsible for any closer linkage between these actions, though, as a matter of fact, most of us will want to make a closer linkage here. For, if we change 'happy Autumn-fields', say, to 'happy April-fields', the two terms tend to draw apart. The fact that the fields are autumn-fields which, though happy, point back to something which is over—which is finished—*does* connect them with the past and therefore properly suggests to the observer thoughts about that past.

To sum up: The first stanza has a unity, but it is not a unity which finds its sanctions in the ordinary logic of language. Its sanctions are to be found in the dramatic context, and, to my mind, there alone. Indeed, the stanza suggests the play of the speaker's mind as the tears unexpectedly start, tears for which there is no apparent occasion, and as he searches for an explanation of them. He calls them 'idle', but, even as he says 'I know not what they mean', he realizes that they must spring from the depths of his being—is willing, with his very next words, to associate them with 'some divine despair'. Moreover, the real occasion of the tears, though the speaker himself comes to realize it only as he approaches the end of the stanza, is the thought about the past. It is psychologically and dramatically right, therefore, that the real occasion should be stated explicitly only within the last line of the stanza.

This first stanza, then, recapitulates the surprise and bewilderment in the speaker's own mind, and sets the problem which the succeeding stanzas are to analyze. The dramatic effect may be described as follows: the stanza seems, not a meditated observation, but a speech begun impulsively—a statement which the speaker has begun before he knows how he will end it.

In the second stanza we are not surprised to have the poet characterize the days that are no more as 'sad,' but there is some shock in hearing him apply to them the adjective 'fresh'. Again, the speaker does not pause to explain: the word 'fresh' actually begins the stanza. Yet the adjective justifies itself.

The past is fresh as with a dawn freshness—as fresh as the first beam glittering on the sail of an incoming ship. The ship is evidently expected; it brings friends, friends 'up from the underworld'. On the surface, the comparison is innocent: the 'underworld' is merely the antipodes, the world which lies below the horizon—an underworld in the sense displayed in old-fashioned geographies with their sketches illustrating the effects of the curvature of the earth. The sails, which catch the light and glitter, will necessarily be the part first seen of any ship which is coming 'up' over the curve of the earth. [...]

If this poem were merely a gently melancholy reverie on the sweet sadness of the past, stanzas II and III would have no place in the poem. But the poem is no such reverie: the images from the past rise up with a strange clarity and sharpness that shock the speaker. Their sharpness and freshness account for the sudden tears and for the psychological problem with which the speaker wrestles in the poem. If the past would only remain melancholy but dimmed, sad but worn and familiar, we should have no problem and no poem. At least, we should not have *this* poem; we should certainly not have the intensity of the last stanza.

—Cleanth Brooks, *The Well-Wrought Urn* (New York: Harcourt, Brace, and Company, 1947): pp. 177–80. ☙

GRAHAM HOUGH ON THE POEM AS A PAGAN EXPRESSION OF DESPAIR AND REGRET

[Graham Hough has written extensively on 18th- and 19th-century British poets and novelists. His critical works include *Reflections on a Literary Revolution* (1960) and *The Romantic Poets* (1953). In the excerpt below, Hough reads the poem as an expression of despair and regret and, in its absence of any elegiac forms of consolation, a pagan poem as well.]

This Tennysonian lyric has been skillfully dissected by Mr. Cleanth Brooks, and its *disjecta membra* added to the rich stock of paradoxes, ironies, and ambiguities boiled up so merrily together in *The Well-Wrought Urn*. What follows is an attempt to put the poem together again.

The theme is an almost objectless regret, rising in the last stanza to something troubled and tumultous. The very slow movement of the opening suggests a heavy and uncontrollable emotion—the spontaneous and unrestrainable welling-up of tears. But it is not a pleasing-melancholy indulgence: the imagery uses all the most poignant suggestions of regret for the irretrievably lost, arranged in a crescendo—autumn fields (happy in themselves, but including the suggestions of lost summer and winter to come), departed friends (the ship disappearing below the horizon), lost life (life beginning again with the birds and the dawn, but lost to the beholder, since he is dying), lost love (the melancholy dead remembering human kisses in the grave; and still more unhappy, the living hopeless lover remembering kisses that once seemed possibilities and are now known to be unattainable). All obvious and powerful sources of irremediable pain—the pathos of autumn, of parting, of death, of hopeless love; all the things that make you cry, suggesting as overtones all the poetry about nostalgia and separation and about being dead when you don't want to be dead:

> O western wind when wilt thou blow,
> That the small rain down can rain?
> Christ that my love were in my arms
> And I in my bed again...

My mouth is full cold, Margaret,
And my breath smells earthy strong.
If you have ae kiss of my clay-cold lips
Your time will not be long . . .

and the ghosts in Virgil stretching out their hands to the farther shore. This is not the elegiac feeling, not like the 'Elegy in a Country Church-yard' or Valéry's 'Cimetière Marin', where the limitations of human life are swallowed up in the will of God of some more metaphysical consolation. Nor is it the romantic commonplace 'I have been half in love with easeful death'. Are we to take the sorrow for 'the days that are no more' in a personal way (last summer when I was happy, the days when my friends were with me, the days when I still thought that she might love me)? I do not think so. I think the poem gets its power over the feelings from the way that these strong and clearly realized individual sources of sorrows are used to suggest another kind of sorrow, more inevitable and more universal. But we shall see.

Formally the poem is remarkable for being rhymeless. Very few people notice this. Yet if such a usual and expected element in a lyric poem is missing there must be some reason; and if people do not notice its absence something must be very skilfully put in to supply its place. If we ask why rhyme is absent, we first have to say why it is usually present. What does rhyme do? Commonly it emphasizes the conventional verse form, by pointing the ends of the lines and so helping to give an effect of completeness and definition. . . .

Why is Death in Life so powerful? Of course they are big words; and the phrase brings to mind 'In the midst of life we are in death'; and Colerige's Life-in-Death in *The Ancient Mariner*. But the first of these is meant to suggest the awful proximity of the Four Last Things—Death, Judgement, Hell, and Heaven; and Coleridge's Life-in-Death symbolizes the *misère de l'homme sans Dieu*—the state of man who is fallen and powerless to save himself without supernatural aid. I think these associations are both wrong here. This is a quite pagan poem. We have already noted the absence of any of the quasi-Christian or supernatural consolations common in elegy. The tears are idle because they spring from despair; a situation you cannot do anything about. (When are tears ever other than idle? They may be useful if they relieve the feelings and leave you free for further action. But no action is going to cure this sorrow.) Despair is a sin in Christian moral theology, and this despair is therefore not divine in the Christian sense, but only in the sense of being something daemonic, some more than personal force, with some more than private cause.

The 'daemonic' suggestion comes up again with the 'underworld' of the second stanza. The primary sense of this is clearly the geographical one of the antipodes, but the suggestion of the classical underworld, the land of the shades, is so strong that it almost swamps the other meaning. But of course Tennyson doesn't really mean an underworld inhabited by ghosts. What does the old symbol stand for in a modern consciousness? Surely for submerged memory from which our friends and other fragments of the past can and sometimes do emerge with such moving and embarrassing freshness. Similarly the next two lines are first a concrete geographical parting, and then the realization that the shades are only shades, that memories are going to disappear again into oblivion. The connection between the coming up of the friends from the underworld and their sinking below the verge is not obvious on the surface; it is only by the secondary meanings—the appearance and disappearance of buried memories—that they are linked. Ghosts appearing from the past—the incursion of the dead into the land of the living.

The same death and life antithesis is in stanza three—the birds waking up and the dawn breaking, the day coming to life, as the man is dying. These lines seem very painful, because the two movements are so utterly out of sympathy with each other: to the man who is dying it is strange that the day should be coming to birth: to the birds and the daylight it is merely indifferent that a man is dying. The words recall too the haunted chilly suspense of the hour before dawn, when vitality is at its lowest: death in life again.

—Graham Hough, "Tears, Idle Tears," *Hopkins Review* (1951). Reprinted in *Critical Essays on the Poetry of Tennyson*, ed. John Killham (New York: Barnes and Noble Books, 1960): pp. 186–89.

LEO SPITZER ON THE DIVINE PRESENCE IN THE POEM

[Leo Spitzer is a very well-known literary critic. His works include *Essays on English and American Literature* (1962) and *Classical and Christian Ideas of World Harmony: Prolo- gomena to an Interpretation of the Word 'Stimmung'* (1963). In the excerpt below, Spitzer responds to Hough's reading of the poem as pagan and, instead, sees the divine presence in the poem as "God Death-in-Life" who will be revealed.]

I must disagree with Mr. Graham Hough's sensitive and thoughtful interpretation of Tennyson's poem 'Tears, Idle Tears'; insofar as he seems, in my opinion, to have failed sufficiently to clarify the nature of the element which Tennyson calls (line 2) 'some divine despair' and which contains the principle on which the structure of the whole poem rests. As for the epithet 'divine', Mr. Hough limits himself to paraphrasing this by 'daemonic' (which term he defines as 'some more than personal force, some more than private cause') and to pointing out a reflection of this daemonic element in the mention of the 'underworld' in the second stanza. According to my own interpretation, 'some divine despair' means quite literally 'the despair of *some God*' (the Latinate use of the adjective instead of a noun in the genitive, is paralleled by the phrase 'the Aeolian harp' = the harp of Aeolus): of a God as yet unnamed, but who will be clearly revealed (and named) in the end of the poem as the God of 'Death in Life'. Our philological interpretation must then, in contrast to the procedure of the poet, start with the definition of the nature and attitude of the deity which is atmospherically ('*some divine despair*') present in the poem from its very beginning. The particular god (or *Sondergott*, to use the classical scholar Usener's term) of Tennyson's making is neither Life nor Death, but Death-in-Life; surely not the Christian deity, as Hough has felt; no more is he Thanatos or Pluto, the God of the underworld before whom man is doomed to appear after death, or even one of the aloof, serene Gods of Epicurus who dwell in the *intermundia*, unconcerned with man. The God Death-in-Life, who, like Christ, has his dwelling-place among the mortals as his name indicates, while sharing the aloofness of the Epicurean Gods, is an impressive and sterile dark God wrapped in his own 'despair' (his *intermundium* is life itself), 'idle' as are the tears of the poet. With the invocation of the name of the God who had been 'somehow' present, or latent, in the poem from the start, the poet's sad 'thinking' has come to an end, but not, we must surmise, his despair and his idle tears. To find a name (or intellectual formula) for the source of our sorrows is not necessarily to free ourselves from their impact. The poem

'Tears, Idle Tears', full of intellectual groping as it is, remains to its end an idle complaint—for the God Death-in-Life who in the end is revealed as the personification of the *lacrimae rerum* will not be able to quench the tears.

And now that I have clarified the 'particular theology' underlying our poem—are our modern critics deaf to the claims of any God?—I would point out that our poem, from beginning to end, is conceived from the point of view both of the 'remembering' poet and of the God 'Death in Life' (for remembrance to our un-Proustian poet is just that: Death in Life). The latter aspect explains, for instance, the order in which the various melancholy pictures of life are enumerated in our poem: in stanza two the first example is that of the sail 'that brings our friends up from the underworld': this is not only a poetic symbol for 'submerged memory from which our friends and other fragments of the past can and do emerge' (Hough), but also the actual vista before the eyes of the God Death-in-Life; he must see both the memory of friendship and the death of friends (next line) only in terms of the to-and-fro movements of Charon's bark. For him friendship is ephemeral, tinged with the mourning of death; for Death-in-Life it is death that is the normal course of events. Again, consider the picture of birds as they awake to life in the morning through song, but who, as seen by our God, awake and sing at the moment when a human being dies. And finally, this god will give precedence, among remembrances of love, to 'remember'd *kisses after death*" 'first love' will appear in the wake of kisses after death and of unhappy love (since, in the view of the dark god and of the melancholy poet, the former must share the mortality of the latter experiences). All the pictures we are offered in our poem—happy autumn fields, friendships, morning birds, first love—are full of brightness on the surface, but suffused with the deep dark shadows of mourning. It is death that is called upon here to interpret life.

—Leo Spitzer, "'Tears, Idle Tears', Again," *Hopkins Review* (1952). Reprinted in *Critical Essays on the Poetry of Tennyson*, ed. John Killham (New York: Barnes and Noble Books, 1960): pp. 192–94.

J. Hillis Miller on the Poem's Conception of Time

[J. Hillis Miller's critical works include *The Linguistic Moment: From Wordsworth to Stevens* (1985) and *William Carlos Williams: A Collection of Critical Essays* (1966). In this excerpt, Miller examines "Tears, Idle Tears" in the context of the volume of poems entitled *The Princess*, of which it is a part. It is, Miller says, a poem that deals with the theme of "poetic thinking"; in other words, it focuses on our need to express experience in terms of time and spatial images.]

We ordinarily distinguish sharply between criticism and poetry. Some poets, we say—Coleridge, Arnold, and T. S. Eliot, for example—were also great critics, but other poets—Shakespeare, Byron, Browning, or Thomas Hardy—were not critics at all or not critics of distinction. We would usually put Tennyson in the latter category. For one thing, he is supposed to have had no aptitude for reflection or for theoretical generalization. W. H. Auden said of Tennyson: "He had the finest ear of any English poet. He was also the stupidest." Tennyson left no body of criticism. . . .

Though "Tears, Idle Tears" has its own integrity, is usually read outside its context, and was probably written without *The Princess* in mind, nevertheless the poem is inserted at a dramatic moment in *The Princess*. The singing of it by one of Princess Ida's "maids" helps precipitate the catastrophe of the poem: the revelation that Princess Ida's female college has been invaded by three men disguised as women. "Tears, Idle Tears" is therefore placed against a background of questions about gender roles and women's liberation. Like Henry James's *The Bostonians*, *The Princess* ends with the triumph of traditional marriage. . . .

For the Princess, who, according to the poem, is wrong about just about everything, time is what it has been in the Western tradition since Plato and St. Augustine. For her, time is a series of presents—past present, present present, and future present. These presents are gathered into one by being all copresent from all time to the *nunc stans* of God. The Princess is right to be affronted by "Tears, Idle Tears," when a little later it is sung, since among other things it expresses a radically different view of time from the traditional one she so glibly expresses. It is impossible to know whether or not Tennyson knew this. His poem, however, speaks for him. It speaks poetically for a view of time as generated by difference, non-presence, distance, unattainability, and loss that can never be made up by a recovered presence in the bosom of God. God, in fact, suffers from a "divine despair" at not being able to recuperate and encompass all the times and places of his creation. By "speaking poetically," I mean speaking through image and rhetorical structure rather than through conceptual formulation. . . .

Associating time with a movement down from heights also prepares for the use of spatial images to express human temporality in "Tears." The up/down axis, however, has a different meaning in the poem: up is this present life and moment, while down is death.

As Heidegger observes in *Sein und Zeit*, the terminology available in Western languages for expressing time is remarkably impoverished. Since we lack adequate specifically temporal language, we Westerners always express time (and falsify it) in some spatial image or other, for example in the movement of the hands of a clock. In fact, however, space is the opening out of time, an opening out that is generated rather than merely registered by language. If there is no proper language for time, then time can only be expressed figuratively, that is, by one or another species of catachresis, through the importation of an improper word where there is no proper one. The project of "Tears, Idle Tears" is to find a way with spatial images to express Tennyson's peculiar apprehension of human time, especially his sense of the past. Tennyson must, that is, try to turn time into language or make time of words. This is both a poetic and a theoretical project. For Tennyson one of the major uses of poetry is to express the human sense of time. This is an example of what I mean when I say Tennyson's critical and theoretical thinking about poetry takes place in his poems, not in prose about poetry.

Temporal distance is associated with spatial distance in the first stanza of "Tears," when the theme of the poem is announced. "[L]ooking on the happy Autumn-fields / And thinking of the days that are no more" makes the speaker of the poem cry, but the tears are idle and without ascertainable meaning. Though the poem is sung by one of the Princess's maidens, no doubt it expresses Tennyson's own obsession with what he called the "passion of the past." Twice in comments about the poem he asserted that it was written at a particular "mouldered lodge" of the past, Tintern Abbey: "This song came to me on the yellowing autumn-tide at Tintern Abbey, full for me of its bygone memories. It is the sense of the abiding in the transient." Tennyson does not mention Wordsworth, but "Tears, Idle Tears" has the same theme as Wordsworth's poem and might almost be called Tennyson's "Tintern Abbey." Among the "bygone memories" was surely this one of Wordsworth's many poems about memory, as well as the memory of the history that is inscribed materially in the ruined abbey. Tennyson insisted, however, that the tears of the poem were not generated by "real woe, as some people might suppose; 'it was rather the yearning that young people occasionally experience for that which seems to have passed away from them for ever.'" This is an important clue. The poem, Tennyson is saying, with however much or little of degeneration, does not express sorrow about separation from any real person, for example his separation by death from Hallam, who is buried not far from the ruins of Tintern Abbey. All the images in the poem about separation from friends and the woe of unfulfilled desire are just that, merely images, prosopopoeias for something that is imageless and has nothing to do with persons. They are images, that is, for human temporality.

—J. Hillis Miller, "Temporal Topographies: Tennyson's Tears," *Victorian Poetry* 30, no. 3–4 (Autumn-Winter 1992): pp. 277–81.

Thematic Analysis of
In Memoriam A.H.H.

In 1833, Alfred Tennyson received the most important letter of his young life. That letter brought the tragic news that Tennyson's dearest and most cherished friend had passed away at the young age of twenty-two, the victim of an attack of ague. (Ague was an illness whose characteristic symptom was regular bouts of fever, chills, and sweating. As Hermione De Almelda states in his book, *Romantic Medicine and John Keats,* medicine at the time of Hallam's death was confused over the phenomenon of fever, referring to it as "an unspecified determination of the blood." It was much feared by physicians of the time.)

Alfred Tennyson was only twenty-four years at the time of Hallam's unexpected and untimely death. He had met Hallam at Cambridge University in April 1829. As Tennyson said in his elegiac tribute to Hallam, "theirs was a sacred bond." With the upcoming marriage of Hallam to Tennyson's sister, Alfred foresaw that their bond would grow even stronger. "Thy blood, my friend, and partly mine; / For now the day was drawing on, / When thou shouldst link thy life with one / Of mine own house and boys of thine."

In Memoriam A.H.H., composed over the course of sixteen or seventeen years (1833–1849), was begun in September 1833, shortly after Hallam's death, and was not published until 1850. It is a poem consisting of small, self-contained poems, 131 stanzas in all, each of which short poems can stand independently as a complete thought. Indeed, Tennyson stated that he did not write these poems with a view of weaving them into a comprehensive work. The poems are not presented according to any chronology of composition; neither does *In Memoriam* contain any unified theme but instead encompasses both personal, political, and philosophical issues relevant to both the poet and the times in which he lived.

Because *In Memoriam* is ostensibly dedicated to the poet's friend and mentor, Arthur Henry Hallam, as we would expect the poem is both a celebration of Hallam's life and a lament for Tennyson's loss of the friend who was his main source of encouragement and inspiration. The poem expresses his search to find a way to handle his feelings of abandonment.

These feelings were not mere literary expressions, for Tennyson did indeed experience a lack of direction and purpose after Hallam died. "To Sleep I give my powers away; / My will is bondsman to the dark; / I sit within a helmless bark." Tennyson felt torn apart, both body and soul, and one of the predominant images through which he expresses those feelings is the marriage metaphor. He compares his own plight to the one who cries the "tears of the widower" and his sister's loss (to whom Hallam was engaged) to that of a grieving widow. "Could we forget the widow'd hours / . . . As on a maiden in the day / When first she wears her orange-flower!"

Along with this recitation of grief and emotion, as always in his work, the poet finds a source of consolation, a way of explaining the loss to himself and achieving a renewed hope for the future. "His credit thus shall set me free; / And, influence-rich to soothe and save, / Unused example from the grave / Reach out dead hands to comfort me." A second personal theme emerges from Tennyson's poetic voice: one aspect of hope's renewal will be the poet's ability to return to his writing, to overcome the emotional barriers that accompany the mourning process, allowing him to recapture the poetic inspiration of former days. "Deep folly! Yet that this could be— / That I could wing my will with might / To leap the grades of life and light / And flash at once, my friend, to thee?"

Because *In Memoriam* does perform the work of mourning, it belongs, in part, to the classical genre of the elegy. The elegy is a type of poem occasioned by the death of a person; it contains certain standard structural parts that include a ceremonial mourning for an exemplary person, praise of his virtues, and, finally, consolation for the loss of the deceased. This particular poetic form can also be used for public purposes, and indeed, Tennyson, who became poet laureate the same year in which *In Memoriam* was published, saw himself in a public capacity, eager to assume his role as poetic and spiritual guide for all of England.

Thus, throughout the entire poem, the personal and the universal are fully intertwined, so much so that personal details take on patriotic meaning. One of the best examples of this transformation of the personal into the political is Tennyson's comparing Hallam to King Arthur, thereby elevating his friend to a mythic dimension. This device places Hallam within the context of the Arthurian legend; Hallam becomes a part of England's literary heritage. "My Arthur whom I shall not see . . . Dear as the mother to the son, / More than my brothers are to me." Tennyson thus bestows upon Hallam the identity of a national hero, granting him epic stature.

An epic poem is defined as an extended narrative, written in a dignified language, which sets forth the story of a people or a nation, with the purpose of memorializing and handing the story down to posterity. Consistent with this genre, Tennyson wrote Hallam into English history and assured himself that both he and his friend will be remembered.

This is the springboard to the poem's larger and more depersonalized agenda. In a far more public and universal context, the poem takes up the theme of humanity's immortality. The poem can be seen as a quest to find justification for human immortality, a journey to work through the doubt and loss of faith that Tennyson saw as the problem of the times in which he lived—the need to "[b]elieve where we cannot prove."

This loss of faith in a divine principle ordering the universe, governing both nature and humanity, came about in the advent of science and secularization. The notion that death, universal to all people, is devoid of any spiritual meaning became commonplace. Instead of the door to heaven, death now meant the absolute end of life's journey. In contrast, Tennyson believed in immortality, most especially an immortality that preserved the integrity of each individual. His was not the medieval concept of humanity's general salvation, a salvation that denied the significance of the individual. In this respect, Tennyson is very much a part of the modern view that recognizes the value of each individual life and believes that individual to be a fitting subject for study. "That each, who seems a separate whole, / Should move his rounds, and fusing all / . . . Remerging in the general Soul."

Science was beginning to challenge long-held beliefs about the origins of life and human progress, precipitating a spiritual crisis—a split between faith and knowledge. Tennyson's response to this division was this: "Let knowledge grow from more to more, / But more of the reverence in us dwell; / That mind and soul, according well, / May make one music as before." This plea to humanity to hold fast to belief in a higher power affirms this higher power's reality, despite all the proliferating scientific theories and explanations for life.

Among the scientific endeavors during the time in which *In Memoriam* was composed was the discovery of the planet Neptune in 1846 and the publication of Sir Charles Lyell's *Principles of Geology,* a book that undermined the biblical story of creation. As Tennyson states in his *Memoirs,* Lyell believed that the lavish profusion of life in the natural world "tells us that God is disease, murder and rapine." But for all their explorations and new explanations concerning humanity and Nature, these theories are by their very nature short-lived, and destined to become quickly obsolete. "Our little systems have their day; / They have their day and cease to be; / They are but broken lifts of thee / And thou, O Lord, art more than they."

What remains, eternal and indestructible, however, is the power of the Word, a gift bestowed on humanity by a divine and loving Creator, and that Word is to be found in the Bible. It contains a power far greater than any poem fashioned by a human being. "And so the Word had breath, and wrought / With human hands the creed of creeds / In loveliness of perfect deeds, / More strong than all poetic thought." And through the medium of words, the poet is finally able to construct an understanding of immortality and a belief in a vital communication with the deceased Hallam. "Yet less of sorrow lives in me / For days of happy commune dead, / Less yearning for the friendship fled / Than some strong bond which is to be."

Thus the poem ends in an Epilogue, Section 131, a celebration of a marriage. Once again it resorts to another classical genre, this one an epithalamion (the Greek word for a wedding song or poem), which was originally intended to be sung on the threshold of the bridal chamber. The marriage described in *In Memoriam* is specifically that of Tennyson's sister Cecilia to Edmund Lushington in 1842. In Tennyson's mind, this new marriage memorialized and celebrated the love between Hallam and Emily Tennyson. Even more, it gave rise to a new-born faith in the poet himself, for it symbolized the promised life to come after death.

Love becomes the binding principle that restores the poet's feeling of wholeness, transcending the ravages of time and Nature. "Regret is dead, but love is more / Than in the summers that are flown, / For I myself with these have grown / To something greater than before." ❀

Critical Views on
In Memoriam A.H.H.

T. S. ELIOT ON THE POEM'S VIRTUOSITY

[T. S. Eliot is a well-known poet and literary critic. Among his most famous works are *The Waste Land* and *Four Quartets*. In the excerpt below, Eliot praises Tennyson's poetic virtuosity. Eliot interprets the poem as a "concentrated diary of a man confessing himself," requiring us to consider the poem only in its entirety.]

It is, in my opinion, in *In Memoriam*, that Tennyson finds full expression. Its technical merit alone is enough to ensure its perpetuity. While Tennyson's technical competence is everywhere masterly and satisfying, *In Memoriam* is the most unapproachable of all his poems. Here are one hundred and thirty-two passages, each of several quatrains in the same form, and never monotony or repetition. And the poem has to be comprehended as a whole. We may not memorize a few passages, we cannot find a 'fair sample'; we have to comprehend the whole of a poem which is essentially the length that it is. We may choose to remember:

> Dark house, by which once more I stand
> Here in the long unlovely street,
> Doors, where my heart was used to beat
> So quickly, waiting for a hand,
>
> A hand that can be clasp'd no more—
> Behold me, for I cannot sleep,
> And like a guilty thing I creep
> At earliest morning to the door.
>
> He is not here; but far away
> The noise of life begins again,
> And ghastly thro' the drizzling rain
> On the bald street breaks the blank day.

This is great poetry, economical of words, a universal emotion on what could only be an English town: and it gives me the shudder that I fail to get from anything in *Maud*. But such a passage, by itself, is not *In Memoriam: In Memoriam* is the whole poem. It is unique: it is a long poem made by putting together lyrics, which have only the unity and continuity of a diary, the concentrated diary of a man confessing himself. It is a diary of which we have to read every word.

Apparently Tennyson's contemporaries, once they had accepted *In Memoriam,* regarded it as a message of hope and reassurance to their rather fading Christian faith. It happens now and then that a poet by some strange accident expresses the mood of his generation, at the same time that he is expressing a mood of his own which is quite remote from that of his generation. This is not a question of insincerity: there is an amalgam of yielding and opposition below the level of consciousness. Tennyson himself, on the conscious level of the man who talks to reporters and poses for photographers, to judge from remarks made in conversation and recorded in his son's Memoir, consistently asserted a convinced, if somewhat sketchy, Christian belief. And he was a friend of Frederick Denison Maurice—nothing seems odder about that age than the respect which its eminent people felt for each other. Nevertheless, I get a very different impression from *In Memoriam* from that which Tennyson's contemporaries seem to have got. It is of a very much more interesting and tragic Tennyson. His biographers have not failed to remark that he had a good deal of the temperament of the mystic—certainly not at all the mind of the theologian. He was desperately anxious to hold the faith of the believer, without being very clear about what he wanted to believe: he was capable of illumination which he was incapable of understanding. The 'Strong Son of God, immortal Love', with an invocation of whom the poem opens, has only a hazy connection with the Logos, or the Incarnate God. Tennyson is distressed by the idea of a mechanical universe; he is naturally, in lamenting his friend, teased by the hope of immortality and reunion beyond death. Yet the renewal craved for seems at best but a continuance, or a substitute for the joys of friendship upon earth. His desire for immortality never is quite the desire for Eternal Life; his concern is for the loss of man rather than for the gain of God.

shall he,

> Man, her last work, who seem'd so fair,
>   Such splendid purpose in his eyes,
>   Who roll'd the psalm to wintry skies,
> Who built him fanes of fruitless prayer,

Who trusted God was love indeed
         And love Creation's final law—
         Tho' Nature, red in tooth and claw
With ravine, shriek'd against his creed—

Who loved, who suffer'd countless ills,
         Who battled for the True, the Just,
         Be blown about the desert dust,
Or seal'd within the iron hills?

—T. S. Eliot, *Essays Ancient and Modern* (London: Faber and Faber, 1936): pp. 211–13.

PATRICK SCOTT ON THE THEME OF ROOTEDNESS AND DISLOCATION IN THE POEM

[Patrick Scott is the author of *Culture and Education in Victorian England* (1990) and editor of *Victorian Poetry 1830 to 1870: An Anthology* (1971). In the excerpt below, Scott discusses the importance of the landscape of Somersby where Tennyson spent both his childhood and early adult life, and offers an alternative elegiac theme to the poet's conflicting experiences of rootedness and dislocation.]

Tennyson writes to Emily Sellwood, perhaps some time in 1838:

> I have dim mystic sympathies with tree and hill reaching far back into childhood. A known landskip is to me an old friend, that continually talks to me of my youth and half-forgotten things, and does more for me than many a friend that I know.

This is a remarkable passage in many ways, not least in its timing and audience. In 1838, Tennyson had recently left, after twenty-eight years of almost continuous residence, the "known landskip" of his Somersby childhood, and as things turned out had left it more or less permanently. The original recipient of the letter was the old friend he would marry, and as time passed she would become almost the sole remaining voice to talk to him of his Lincolnshire youth. And the mystic significance of "tree and hill" reverberates through so many lines of *In Memoriam* that this letter's privileging of landscape over friendship, and its linking of landscape with the amnesiac insecurities of a migratory adulthood, might make one reread Tennyson's poem as elegizing not a person, Arthur Hallam, but a place, Lincolnshire, or rather as elegizing what place itself had come to represent for Tennyson and his early Victorian contemporaries. We can best tease out this broader theme of local rootedness and uprootedness in Tennyson's writing and generation by reexamining the treatment of geographical dislocation in *In Memoriam* itself. . . .

Tennyson married a Lincolnshire woman he had known since before Hallam's death. Their servants after marriage came from Lincolnshire. He retained a Lincolnshire accent all his life. But after the family left Somersby in 1837, he never went back for any extended period. He looked for a married home in the Lake District, Malvern, Sussex, Kent, almost anywhere except Lincolnshire. Late in life he passed up the opportunity to buy the Somersby estate for his son Hallam. Even his peerage was gazetted to not one, but two, locations in counties other than Lincolnshire. . . . Tennyson experienced and internalized a radical cultural disjunction or dislocation, symbolized by his attitude to Somersby, a dislocation that late Victorian fans like Walters or Napier or the Rawnsleys were trying to reserve or deny.

Now the study of place in Tennyson is significant because his experience of place and displacement, rootedness and uprootedness, was paradigmatic for a whole generation, and indeed became culturally normative for generations afterwards. The shifting nineteenth-century vocabulary of place—origin, locality, region, provinciality, cosmopolitanism, and so on—marks the cultural shifts and insecurities of the period, quite as much as those idealist high-cultural vocabularies that effaced poetic topography. And there are sound historical reasons why Tennyson's own geographical uprooting resonated so strongly with his contemporaries. The nineteenth century saw an enormous increase, not just in emigration overseas, but in internal migration, as changed agricultural practices, urban expansion, and improved inland transportation made physcial and social uprooting the normative experience for the majority of Britons. . . .

What we may call the topographical narrative of *In Memoriam* may be easily surveyed, but it is more subtly influenced than, under Romantic influence, we have commonly assumed. The opening segment of the poem is set firmly in Lincolnshire, dealing with a loss elsewhere; it covertly takes for granted that Tennyson knows where he is, that the "real life" threatened by Hallam's death-in-absence is being lived in a known landskip. The first churchyard section (section 2) is patently not about Hallam's grave but about Tennyson finding *his* identity lying, not within himself, but in the familiarities of near-pagan village fatalism. His impatient dialogue with the commonplace "cultured" responses to Hallam's death is a response to correspondents living elsewhere (section 6), or to passing travelers, the classical viator or wayfarer (section 21). The reality of Tennyson's bereavement is articulated locally, within the rectory family, in consciousness of the younger sister who now must forsee perpetual maidenhood. It is no accident that *In Memoriam*'s first set-piece landscape section is also one of the great anthology-sections for Tennyson's Lincolnshire fans:

> Calm and deep peace on this high wold,
>> And on these dews that drench the furze,
>> And all the silvery gossamers
> That twinkle into green and gold:

. . . This initial taken-for-granted topographical footing gives way to a poem that is all over the place, yet Somersby provides one of the continuing benchmarks for the poem's progression—the succession of family Christmases. These Christmases delineate Tennyson's emerging sense of his experience as ambiguous, limiting, provincial, rather than as the valorized local origin of his Romantic predecessors, and his regionalist successors. . . . *In Memoriam*'s first Christmas is the most deeply conflicted, symbolized in the punning status of the wreaths the family weaves for house and church, at once funereal and mockingly festive, a "vain pretence of gladness." It is a conflict with a very localized setting, in the close village network to the south wolds. The Christmas bells that answer each other are "four voices of four hamlets round / From far and near, or mead and moor," and Tennyson resents how much these "merry merry bells of Yule" stil rule his "troubled spirit," "for they controlled me when a boy" (section 28). Provincial origins, like family responsibilities, are there, at the end of *In Memoriam*'s first segment, both coercive and in some degrees resented; the Christmas games are "vain pretence of gladness" (section 30).

By the second Christmas, more briefly narrated, the family has repressed its grief, but Tennyson himself stands half outside the process of regional recuperation. He now sees the revival of "our ancient games" as perhaps saving fictions. The "mimic pictures" of the tableaux are valued because the actors are alive and not the statues they pretend; the central synedoche is a game of blindman's bluff, or, as Tennyson threateningly calls it, "hoodman's [i.e., hangman's] blind," where a seeing subject willingly makes himself unable to see for the sake of familial cohesion, but still stands ready to strike or make captive unpredictably (section 78).

And with the third Christmas, the poem's decentering from Lincolnshire and family origin has become literalized, with the Tennysons' move from Somersby to High Beach. Now a single unfamiliar Essex church replaces the four close wold hamlets; "these are not the bells I know":

> Like strangers' voices here they sound
> In lands where not a memory strays
> Nor landmark breathes of other days
> But all is new unhallowed ground. (104.8–12)

—Patrick Scott, "Tennyson, Lincolnshire, and Provinciality: The Topographical Narrative of *In Memoriam*," *Victorian Poetry* 34, no. 1 (Spring 1996): pp. 39, 41–44.

JOHN D. ROSENBERG ON PERSONAL EXPERIENCE AND SOCIAL CONCERNS IN THE POEM

[John D. Rosenberg is the author of *The Fall of Camelot: A Study of Tennyson's "Idylls of the King"* (1973). In the excerpt below, Rosenberg discusses the way in which the poet combines both personal experience and contemporary social concerns in *In Memoriam* and *Idylls of the King* to create a poetry in which hopelessness and optimism coexist.]

The roots of that hyper-realism go back to Tennyson's earliest childhood. Born in 1809, Tennyson spent his first eighteen years in the family home at Somersby, a remote village in Lincolnshire. His heredity, his temperament, above all the morbidly intense family relationships of the Tennysons, seemed calculated to convey to his senses a world at once menacing and sublime, shadowy and solid, crowded yet achingly solitary. One of eleven siblings, two of whom went mad, Tennyson grew up in the shadow of his violently melancholic and alcoholic father, the Reverend Dr. George Clayton Tennyson. Life in the isolated rectory at Somersby was at once cultured and eccentric, authoritarian and wild. . . . The "black blood" of the Tennysons is no melodramatic invention of the poet's biographers but an anxious legacy that shadowed Tennyson's life and haunts much of his poetry. The strife of kin, violence, melancholy, suicide, madness, and death figure more or less prominently in virtually all of his greatest poems. . . .

For us, in whose eyes our Victorian grandfathers appear far more complex and sympathetic than they did to our own fathers, there is no need to invent a Tennyson divided against himself or in subversive hostility to his period. In his strengths as in his weaknesses, in his fears, hates, loves, and hopes, Tennyson is remarkably representative of his time; he had no more need to deceive himself than to deceive his contemporaries. Dreams, madness, doubt, suicide, and death *are* very much Tennyson's themes, but they figure as prominently in his later poetry, when he was Laureate, as in his earlier. Sexual obsession and hallucination are as much at the imaginative heart of *Idylls of the King* as of "Mariana" or "The Lotos-Eaters." . . .

To the serious modern reader, then, Tennyson no longer seems an escapist or purveyor of Victorian platitudes. Such a reader recognizes within the period, as within Tennyson's poetry itself, the anxious coexistence of despair and optimism; he detects the skepticism of science as well as deep religious faith, glorification of "progress" alongside impassioned nostalgia for the past, materialism as well as mysticism, robust self-assertion alongside much fear and trembling. "What am I," Tennyson exclaims in *In Memoriam*, but

> An infant crying in the night;
> An infant crying for the light,
> And with no language but a cry.   (LIV, 18–20)

The shock that evolutionary science posed to Christian faith was as devastating to the Victorians as the dread of nuclear holocaust is to us. That annihilating shock is nowhere more feelingly or profoundly voiced than in *In Memoriam*, published a decade before Darwin's *The Origin of Species*. The tense dialogue of faith in mortal combat with doubt makes *In Memoriam* the archetypically Victorian poem. Yet Tennyson's elegy to his friend Arthur Hallam is also intensely personal, indeed one of the greatest love poems in English. Paradoxically, this most private of Tennyson's utterances is also his most public poem; Queen Victoria so admired *In Memoriam*, published in 1850, that she appointed Tennyson Poet Laureate.

As Tennyson recedes from us in time, he moves closer to us in spirit; we now see that we are the heirs of his perplexities and fears, if not of his hopes. Although the period of unreflective hostility to Tennyson has passed, we are in danger of falling into an opposite excess: seeing in his poetry the mirror of our own preoccupations and embracing not Tennyson himself, but the flattering phantom of our own predispositions. Tennyson was attracted to, and fought fiercely against, the seductions of the aberrant, the violent, the irrational. Above all, he was haunted and appalled by the corrosively voluptuous desire for death. . . .

The current bias of Tennyson criticism overstresses the darker half of his dialectic, the voice of doubt, illusion, surrender, and death. Thus *In Memoriam*, once rejected as a simplistic assertion of faith, is now in peril of being stood on its head and praised as an existential cry of total despair. Yet the poem is not about the triumph of doubt over faith or of faith over doubt, but rather explores the tensions and strange affinities between the two. So, too, *Idylls of the King*, long dismissed as a medieval charade, is now in danger of being resurrected as a prophecy of nihilistic extinction. Such a one-sided reading reflects the modern transvaluation that has resulted in the fad of doom, an infatuation with apocalypse, a beatification of the ugly and the irrational that Tennyson would have found abhorrent and incomprehensible. He never denied the threat to reason or civilization—humanity itself reels back into bestiality in King Arthur's fatal Last Battle—but he never assumed that their doom was foreordained or took perverse comfort in the romance of annihilation. Significantly, the three most precious gifts that Pallas can offer Paris in "Oenone" are "self-reverence, self-knowledge, self-control." Paris spurns all three, with disastrous consequences to Troy and to civilization. One senses that Tennyson prized those gifts so highly because he feared so keenly the horrors of self-delusion and self-degradation.

—John D. Rosenberg, "Tennyson and the Landscape of Consciousness," *Victorian Poetry* 12, no. 4 (Winter 1974): pp. 304–307.

DONALD S. HAIR ON THE DISTINCTION BETWEEN SOUL AND SPIRIT

[Donald S. Hair has written extensively on the Victorian poets. His critical works include *Browning's Experiments with Genre* (1972) and *Domestic and Heroic in Tennyson's Poetry* (1981). In the excerpt below, Hair does a close reading of the distinction between soul and spirit, in which soul has already been created for us while spirit is the living principle, a passing breeze, that enables us to imagine, interpret, and create. Spirit becomes the poet's goal in this elegy—to shape and interpret the world.]

Tennyson uses the words "soul" and "spirit" frequently and confidently in *In Memoriam,* but late twentieth-century readers are likely to find the words slightly embarrassing, and to feel less than confident of Tennyson's meaning. My own experience of the response to these words has been mainly in the classroom, and I know that students, undergraduates and graduates both, think that "soul" and "spirit" are synonyms, and that they refer to some vague thing or state that is invisible, immaterial, and largely unknowable. Yet the words are crucial in Tennyson's elegy, from his desire at the beginning to restore "mind and soul" to "one music as before" (Prologue), to his resolve at the end to dwell "in my spirit" (123), and to his hope, expressed in the elegy's final section, of closing "with all we loved, / And all we flow from, soul in soul" (131). My purpose in this paper is to examine the ways in which Tennyson actually uses "soul" and "spirit" in the poem, and to do so in the context of St. Paul's first epistle to the Corinthians, where he distinguishes between the "natural body" and the "spiritual body," and where he suggests the kind of perception proper to each. Tennyson too ultimately distinguishes between the two modes of being, and the kind of perception proper to each is central to the movement and resolution of his elegy. . . .

In contrast to the dualism of the soul-body, the "spiritual body" is a unit. In an important parenthesis, Frye writes, "Paul means that it is a body, not that it *has* one," and it is "an element in us that enables us to understand the scripture and other aspects of revelation."

The distinction between the soul-body and she spiritual body is distinction between two kinds of seeing. "The natural man receiveth not the things of the Spirit of God," Paul writes, "for they are foolishness unto him: neither can he know them, because they are spiritually discerned. But he that is spiritual judgeth all things" (1 Corinthians 2.14–15). The passage is a commonplace in Christian teaching, so it is not surprising to find Tennyson parodying it in an 1833 letter to James Spedding, when he writes merrily about "the recollections of the many intellectual, spirituous, and spiritual evenings we have spent together in olden days—evenings, when spiritual things were spirituously discerned." There is no such parody in *In Memoriam,* where spiritual discernment is the goal and the question of its authority is the poet's concern. Parallels and allusions to Paul's epistle are, as we shall see, crucial parts of the elegy. The first step toward spiritual discernment involves a rejection of the seeing of the "natural man." . . .

In spite of Tennyson's blurring the difference between "soul" and "spirit" in the early sections of the poem, a difference is nonetheless discernible, and could perhaps be summed up by grammatical metaphors: "soul" is a past participle (created) while "spirit" is a present participle (creating). We know that we did not create ourselves, but we also know that there is something in us which enables us to make sense of ourselves and the world in which we live. Making sense involves consciousness, imagination, interpretation and, in Tennyson's scheme of things, love. Imagination is among the earliest of these indications of spiritual discernment to become active.

In the initial sections of the poem, the imagination acts in the absence of sensation or physical evidence. In section 17, for instance, which is about the voyage of the ship bearing Hallam's body back to England, the poet follows the vessel's movement, he tells us, with his spirit. He begins by imaging the physical breeze that "Compelled by canvas," and links it with his own prayer, likened to a physical breeze also: it was "as the whisper of an air / To breathe thee over lonely seas" (ll. 3–4). Having introduced the actual breeze, and having troped it through his simile, Tennyson suggests the conventional metaphor in the first line of the second quatrain: "For I in spirit saw thee move." "Spirit" here means the power of one's imagination, understood in the seventeenth-century sense as the ability to image things once perceived but now absent or hidden from the senses. (Hence Hobbes asserts that imagination "is nothing but decaying sense.") By the time we get to section 55, such perception by the spirit no longer depends upon previous sensible experience. There the wish for immortality, in the face of the contrary evidence of nature, derives from "the likest God within the soul" (l. 4). The "likest God" is, I think, spirit, which shapes and interprets its world, though that interpretation is often at odds with the evidence of one's physical sight. This lyric, like the following one, contrasts physical sight, which observes only a separate and alien nature, and another kind of sight, whose center of authority is not in the observed but in the observer, not in one's material existence but in one's genuinely human (that is spiritual) nature. . . .

For the "natural man," immortality manifests itself only as an insubstantial appearance, a ghost. Ghosts haunt the poet's strivings to image Hallam after death, and sometimes appear, by default, after moments of genuine spiritual perception. The attempt of the "natural man" to image Hallam after death in section 70 is rewarded with nightmarish appearances: "Cloud-towers by ghostly masons wrought," "pallèd shapes," and "puckered faces." The will, as Tennyson treats it here, operates in the physical world, and can produce only "hollow masks." "Beyond the will" is another kind of seeing, that of the "spiritual body," which preserves Hallam substantially and bodily: "And through a lattice on the soul / Looks thy fair face and makes it still." Hallam's spiritual body is also his name, proper names being, in Tennyson's scheme of things, one with the individual's uniqueness. . . .

Such a move toward spiritual discernment is an important part of the growth or development or progress of the individual, the kind of change Tennyson was drawing attention to when he considered calling the poem "The Way of the Soul." In this pattern, beings created by God ("souls") are themselves creators ("spirits"), shaping their own natures and the world around them, and participating in essential ways in the move of all things toward the "one far-off divine event" (Epithalamium, l. 143). In this context, Hallam is the "noble type / Appearing ere the times were ripe" (Epithalamium, ll. 138–139), and Tennyson characteristically explores the relation between a lower being (himself) and a higher (Hallam). Both beings are sometimes souls and sometimes spirits, as Tennyson uses the nouns interchangeably.

—Donald S. Hair, "Soul and Spirit in *In Memoriam*," *Victorian Poetry* 34, no. 2 (Summer 1996): pp. 175–79.

KERRY MCSWEENEY ON NATURE'S HEALING EFFECT IN THE POEM

[Kerry McSweeney has written extensively on Victorian poets and novelists. McSweeney's critical works include *George Eliot (Marian Evans): A Literary Life* (1991) and *Tennyson and Swinburne as Romantic Novelists* (1981). In the excerpt below, McSweeney focuses on the healing aspects of nature, as evidenced in the cyclical changes of the seasons, which ultimately allow Tennyson to recover from the loss of Hallam and, indeed, to recapture Hallam's living spirit.]

An important feature of *In Memoriam*, which has not received the attention it deserves, is the poem's pattern of natural consolation. Much attention has been paid to the religious aspects of the poem, of which its intellectual and scientific concerns are clearly a part, but not enough emphasis has been laid on what may be called the naturalism of *In Memoriam*. Perhaps one reason for this relative neglect has been that an examination of the poem's pattern of natural consolation raises some difficult questions about the unity of the poem, and about a—perhaps unresolved—tension in the poem between a naturalistic acceptance of death and a deep-rooted need for belief in an afterlife. It is not my intention in the following discussion to speak to these questions, but one matter which touches directly upon them will have to be carefully examined: the nature of section XCV, a section often taken by commentators to be *In Memoriam*'s most crucial single section, and in several respects its climax.

One of the literary traditions upon which *In Memoriam* draws is that of pastoral elegy. A number of the conventions of this genre appear in the poem, such as the fiction of the poet as a shepherd lamenting his dead mate, the celebration of the idyllic time of shared friendship before the disaster, the invocation to the muses, and the choice of flowers. In addition, there are in the poem echoes of earlier elegies. . . .

More importantly, the general pattern of *In Memoriam* closely follows that of pastoral elegy. There is the initial expression of sorrow and grief, recollection of the happy days now past, troubled reflections on the meaning and purpose of human existence, questioning of the powers in the universe that have allowed so gifted a man to die, the gradual tempering of grief into resignation, the sudden turn or change, through which the poet realizes that his dead friend has not totally perished but survives in some other form, and the apotheosis, which describes the form of this survival and joyfully celebrates it. . . .

It is a commonplace to say that Tennyson, like other Victorian writers, lacked the secure religious faith of earlier centuries and could no longer find support for his need to believe in the traditional sanctions of such faith. The closing sections of *In Memoriam* in consequence offer a variety of consolations and apotheoses, but ones which are not necessarily compatible with each other. There is the domestic epiphany of the epilogue, with its detailed anticipation of a marriage celebration and its confident anticipation of the new life which will result from this union. This epiphany functions in effect as a positive resolution of the various incidents of middle-class tragedy and sadness scattered through the poem. In the pealing of the wild new year's bells in section CVI there is heard the prophecy of a political and social millenium, which is closely associated with the survival of Hallam's spirit. . . .

I do, however, want to call attention to another consolation which flowers in *In Memoriam*'s closing section and which has its roots earlier in the poem. The pattern of natural consolation is perhaps not so prominent or noticeable as other patterns in the poem, but it is no less important and worthy of remark. One reason why this pattern seems less dominant is that it does not culminate in an apotheosis, but completes itself much less spectacularly on a merely natural level, with Tennyson's initial separation from the natural process of cyclic change finally giving way to a most moving identification with it.

Another reason is that there are two quite separate "natures" present in *In Memoriam* which have not been sufficiently distinguished. One is Nature with the capital-*N*, which was the discovery of nineteenth-century science, an abstraction contemplated by Tennyson with much apprehension. This is the "phantom" Nature of III, "A hollow form with empty hands," and the "Nature, red in tooth and claw / With ravine" which so appalls Tennyson in LVI. The other nature is simply the immemorial sights and sounds of the English landscape, the world of seasonal change, and the daily passage from light to dark. . . .

For roughly the first half of *In Memoriam*, references to nature serve mainly to underline Tennyson's isolating grief, which has cut him off from any rapport with natural process. The day of Hallam's death is said to have "sickened every living bloom, / And blurred the splendour of the sun" (LXXII), while XXXVIII states simply that "No joy the blowing season gives." The stasis of grief and the process of nature appear incompatible. In II, it is only within the bleak and solitary yew tree, its roots reaching down into the coffined bones of a corpse, that Tennyson is able to associate himself. In XXXIX it is said that a "golden hour" of bloom comes even to this tree, but this state is short-lived and seems unnatural. The abiding condition of the yew is a barren darkness, implicit even in its transitory blossoms: "Thy gloom is kindled at the tips, / And passes into gloom again." In LXIX the poet dreams "there would be spring no more," and in LIV he has only the faintest of hopes that, like the turning of the seasons, his grief too will eventually change:

> I can but trust that good shall fall
> At last—far off—at last, to all,
> And every winter change to spring.

. . . Shortly after the second Christmas section (LXXVIII), which A. C. Bradley rightly regarded as the "turning point in the general feeling of *In Memoriam*," there are three lovely poems in which a decided change in Tennyson's relation to the natural world is to be noted. These are poems of petition and invocation, which ask different aspects of the restorative force of natural process to bring to bear on the poet's grief their powers of assuagement and revivification. LXXXIII appeals to the new year not to delay but to bring on the "sweetness" of spring: "Can trouble live with April days, / Or sadness in the summer moons?" The changes of the earth will produce a corresponding change inside the poet:

> O thou, new-year, delaying long,
>> Delayest the sorrow in my blood,
>> That longs to burst a frozen bud
> And flood a fresher throat with song.

—Kerry McSweeney, "The Pattern of Natural Consolation in *In Memoriam*," *Victorian Poetry* 11, no. 2 (Summer 1993): pp. 87–91.

Thematic Analysis of
"The Passing of Arthur"

"The Passing of Arthur," originally entitled "Morte d'Arthur," was published in its final form and current title in 1869. It is the last poem from Tennyson's collection of poems entitled *Idylls of the King,* a project which he spent some 55 years writing and revising. Both the title of this individual poem and the general title *Idylls of the King* place the poem within two important literary contexts: first, the birth and death of King Arthur and the Knights of the Round Table as written by Sir Thomas Malory in 1485 in his *Morte d'Arthur,* and second, the idyll, a classical genre of poetry, which was a brief yet artful representation of contemporary life, describing a scene in great detail or narrating an actual story, that dated back to Theocritus in the third century B.C. Thus, the literary background of this poem merits consideration in order to appreciate Tennyson's efforts to experiment with and rework literature from a distant past. Tennyson does this to make a statement about the times in which he lived, the England of Queen Victoria, whose reign spanned almost seven decades, from 1837 until her death in 1901.

The Arthurian romance is an elaborately constructed collection of stories depicting an ideal society of fellowship among the knights of the Round Table. Indeed, the very concept of a round table is significant, as it was intended that King Arthur would be seated in a circular fashion with all of his faithful knights, an arrangement in which all were literally placed with equal status and standing, a true democracy. The knights were required to demonstrate an unfailing loyalty to their King and had sworn by oath to defend the kingdom of Camelot unto death. They were required to live by a code of bravery and honor—a code known as chivalry. This code also grew into an elaborate literary construction where the chivalrous knight was committed to a lifelong service of women, an art of courtly love that required defending the woman's honor.

The Arthurian romance is a legend, which is to say that it is loosely based on historical fact and greatly embellished by poets and writers of imaginary works. While there is some evidence for a historical King Arthur, who is believed to have been a British or Roman-British leader who resisted the Anglo-Saxon invaders of sixth-century England, it is the legendary Arthur, the center of the Round Table and the most exemplary of the chivalrous knights, who is so important to literature.

This legend has been growing for centuries, each era finding new life and meaning in the old stories. Malory himself adapted the story of Camelot from a variety of French romances that flourished during the 12th century. Tennyson used the Arthurian legend to explore many contemporary social and artistic concerns, among them true and false love, as well as the rise and fall of a society founded on principles and equality.

In Malory's version of the Arthurian romance, Tennyson must have heard echoes of his own unhappy home life. The *Morte d'Arthur* portrayed the endangered state of childhood within the world of Camelot. Malory's Camelot is a place where children must bear the sins of the fathers, a world in which the natural loving relationship between parent and child has been ruptured. Children are alienated and estranged from their parents and this total rupture of the familial bond will eventually prove fatal to the very existence of Arthur and his knights. "For in tho dayes the sonne spared not the fadir no more than a straunger."

The theme of broken family ties lies in the very beginning of the Arthurian legend, the seeds being planted in the illegitimate circumstances of Arthur's own birth. Uther Pendragon, Arthur's father, enters into a bargain with the magician Merlin that if Merlin will magically help him to beget a child, he will deliver that child to Merlin for his upbringing. As part of that bargain, Merlin causes Uther to lie with Igrayne before he marries her, in fact only three hours after the death of her own husband, circumstances which cause Arthur great trouble later on when he tries to claim his inheritance. The untimeliness and illegitimacy of Arthur's conception thus foreshadows the inevitable destruction of the Arthurian world and serves as a backdrop for the internal strife amongst the once ideal fellowship of the Knights of the Round Table.

As far as the classical background is concerned, an "idyllic" poem was part of a convention of pastoral poetry, a work that again, like the Arthurian legend, depicts an ideal portrait of rural life in an imaginary Golden Age, the central theme being the lives and loves of shepherds and shepherdesses. It is also important to note that the intention of these poems varied, sometimes presenting romantic or sentimental views of life, lamenting the loss or death of a loved one, and at other times making a political or social statement. During the Renaissance, the pastoral was further developed into the elegy or poem of mourning and included a statement of grief, as well as inquiry into the cause of death, the sympathy and weeping of Nature, and a procession of mourners. It ended with grief's consolation as the poet finds some higher purpose for the loss of the loved one.

Some of Tennyson's well-known contemporaries did not appreciate his achievement in *Idylls of the King*. Thomas Carlyle described the poems as "lollipops," and Mathew Arnold continued in this vein by stating that *Idylls of the King* is "deficient in intellectual power." Later on, however, such critics as Alfred North Whitehead, in his essay "Science and the Modern World," showed an appreciation for Tennyson, stating that the poet grappled with the complexities of his times, namely the rise of science and a mechanical theory of nature, which contributed to a loss of faith and spiritual purpose.

Tennyson's use of an idealized past is both a commentary on the problems of modern life in the 19th century and a wish for spiritual healing. The harmony he seeks, however, in the final analysis exists only in its ideal form as a literary device. Nevertheless, this ideal society served as a model for his times, a goal toward which its members could be forever striving. In other words, the shaping of the ideal world is never complete; it is always a work in progress.

"The Passing of Arthur" begins and ends with the story of Sir Bedivere, "[f]irst made and latest left of all the knights," and Bedivere shares the responsibility of narrating the story, both what he overhears Arthur saying and the dialogue in which he and Arthur engage, with the poet narrator, who intervenes to provide commentary throughout. The two largest themes of the poem are internecine warfare, a war in which family members are fighting one another ("[a]nd all whereon I lean'd in wife and friend / Is traitor to my peace, and all my realm / Reels back into the beast, and is no more") and, as a consequence of that familial warfare, the undermining of the very foundation upon which society can stand. Both of these themes are also found in Malory.

"The Passing of Arthur" is like an architectural structure, with Arthur's eventual death at the end described as a collapsed pillar, "[s]o like a shatter'd column lay the King; / Not like that Arthur who . . . Shot thro' the lists at Camelot," no longer able to sustain the heavy burden of a fractured world. This very lack of a spiritual foundation is the inaugural event in the poem, with Arthur lamenting his inability to find God among his men. "I mark'd Him in the flowering of His fields / But in His ways with men I find Him not." Arthur offers two possible reasons for his inability to see God—either the world is ruled by "some lesser god" or, as will be proven throughout the poem, the world as God's creation is perfect, "[b]ut that these eyes of men are dense and dim." Failure to see, the loss of faith, has caused the spiritual blindness in Tennyson's poem, and throughout "The Passing of Arthur" images abound of cloudiness and blurred vision. Likewise, the world's inability to see a purpose beyond the present life will all insure that the death of Arthur will be the death of an ideal. " . . . [D]oth all that haunts the waste and wild / Mourn knowing it will go along with me?"

A small but significant detail in "The Passing of Arthur" is Tennyson's use of archaic words, old-fashioned or obsolete words, that evoke the mood of an earlier time. These words are found in Malory and other sources of the medieval legend, words such as "dolorous," meaning that which causes pain and grief.

In the opening stanzas of the poem, Arthur has a dream in which Gawain is killed and Sir Bedivere responds that it is Mordred who is to blame, while counseling the King to "[a]rise, go forth and conquer as of old." Arthur's response to Sir Bedivere is that the true reason for this battle is the loss of high purpose in former days. "Far other is this battle . . . when we strove in youth, / . . . Or thrust the heathen from the Roman wall." And this noble-minded purpose is contrasted with the poet's own, as symbolized by Arthur's current predicament that he cannot engage in battle. Indeed, Arthur is in an untenable position, a position in which he cannot possibly win, and that situation leaves him powerless to enter the fray of internecine warfare, declaring that "[t]he king who fights his people fights himself" (l. 72)

In the next stanza, the image of society's lost foundations is read into the landscape. "Where fragments of forgotten peoples dwelt, /

And the long mountains ended in a coast / Of ever-shifting sand."
In fact, the most important loss of spirituality in a kingdom of "ever-shifting sand" is the loss of memory. In the Middle Ages, society felt a vital ethical responsibility to remember the dead, but in Tennyson's day, the memory of past civilization is no longer a part of society's present world.

This emphasis on memory combines with the wish for a faith in something beyond what is visible to mortal eyes. The narrator searches for a divine purpose to the seemingly inexplicable, a promise of reward in the next life. In "The Passing of Arthur," Tennyson imposes this promise of divine purpose in the words of Arthur to Sir Bedivere: "Pray for my soul. More things are wrought by prayer / Than this world dreams of" (ll. 415–16). ❀

Critical Views on
"The Passing of Arthur"

FRANCIS BERTRAM PINION ON THE AUTOBIOGRAPHICAL CONTEXT OF THE POEM

[Francis Bertram Pinion is the author of several books on Victorian and Romantic writers, including *A George Eliot Companion: A Literary Achievement and Modern Significance,* and *A Tennyson Companion,* from which the following excerpt is taken. Pinion gives an autobiographical context for "The Morte d'Arthur," suggesting that Hallam's death signaled the end of the Round Table.]

Though the reference to twelve books with 'faint Homeric echoes' in its apologetic framework ('The Epic') is fictional, 'Morte d'Arthur' seems to have been designed as a part of a work which might have been continued before the inception of *Idylls of the King* had Tennyson received the encouragement he would have liked. Its wider imaginative implications (the change from Malory's summer to winter, for instance) were such that he was able to incorporate it in the final book of the *Idylls* with no more than the substitution of 'So' for 'And' and the omission of a line made redundant by the new context. The opening line, 'So all day long the noise of battle rolled', suggests an epic continuation at least as heroic as that recalled in 'Ulysses' by 'Far on the ringing plains of windy Troy'. One of Tennyson's most finished works, 'Morte d'Arthur' accommodates classicisms and archaisms with ease; its blank-verse rhythms vary dramatically in speech and in descriptions which are fully accordant to action and scene. In wealth of pictorial and sound effects, its splendours range from the sparkling brilliance of Excalibur to the 'long glories' of the winter moon above the level lake, the serenity of this scene giving sudden antithesis to the clash of Bedivere's armour among echoing cliffs, as he makes his way along 'juts of slippery crag' that ring 'Sharp-smitten with the dint of armèd heels'. Much was drawn from Malory in expression as well as in substance, but the finest effects are Tennyson's, the shriek of the queens becoming hauntingly evocative:

> A cry that shivered to the tingling stars,
> And, as it were one voice, an agony
> Of lamentation, like a wind, that shrills
> All night in a waste land, where no one comes,
> Or hath come, since the making of the world.

'Merlin and the Gleam' shows that Tennyson had Hallam's death in mind when he wrote this epic scene or epyllion: 'Arthur had vanished I knew not whither, The king who loved me, And cannot die'. Bedivere speaks for the poet: 'the days darken round me'. The shock of Hallam's death to the Apostles is alluded to in the dissolution of the Round Table, and the inscrutability of fate, in 'God fulfills himself in many ways'. Arthur's remarks on the efficacy of prayer arise from Ulyssean statements: 'For what are men better than sheep or goats That nourish a blind life within the brain, If, knowing God, they lift not hands of prayer. . . ?' 'The Epic' ends with Christmas bells that, like those in *In Memoriam* (cvi), ring out war and ring in peace.

In the delights of creative artistry such as those of 'Morte d'Arthur', as well as in the 'measured language' of those brief elegies with which *In Memoriam* began, Tennyson was able to numb his sorrow and bring relief to 'the unquiet heart and brain'. 'Over the dark world flies the wind' almost certainly expresses his distress at the time, and conforms strikingly to the pattern of *In Memoriam* poems where feelings are externalized in the natural scene. The disguise is faint in 'Oh! that 'twere possible', after its rather unsatisfactory extension for inclusion in *The Tribute*. The poet is haunted by a shadow, and the fact that it is 'Not thou, but like to thee' makes him cry out, 'Ah God! that it were possible For one short hour to see The souls we loved, that they might tell us What and where they be.' He sees the shadow in the 'silent woody places' around his birthplace; it haunts him in the great city, and makes him half-dreaming of meeting and happy laughter on the morrow, only for him to find in the shuddering dawn that the 'abiding phantom' is cold.

—Francis Bertram Pinion, *A Tennyson Companion* (New York: St. Martin's Press, 1984): pp. 99–100.

[Clyde de L. Ryals is the author of several books on the Victorian and Romantic period, including *A World of Possibilities: Romantic Irony in Victorian Literature,* and *Theme and Symbol in Tennyson's Poems to 1850,* from which this extract was taken. Ryals aruges that Bedivere is an essentially modern man who, even when he finally does obey King Arthur, does so without any belief in a higher principle.]

Bedivere is commanded to fling Excalibur into the mere, but like modern man, deluded by materialism, Bedivere rationalizes his act in refusing to cast the beautiful sword away. He is without faith and denies his vows of obedience to his king, proving unworthy just when he is needed most. After his second failure to perform the deed which his kind commands, Arthur charges him:

> I see thee what thou art,
> For thou, the latest-heft of all my knights,
> In whom should meet the offices of all,
> Thou wouldst betray me for the precious hilt;
> Either from lust of gold, or like a girl
> Valuing the giddy pleasure of the eyes.
> Yet, for a man may fail in duty twice,
> And the third time may prosper, get thee hence.

The third time Bedivere does as he is bidden, but still he performs without faith.

When Excalibur is returned to its rightful place, a funeral barge comes to fetch Arthur, and here appears the ominous imagery once again. On the decks of the barge are

> stately forms
> Black-stoled, black-hooded, like a dream—by these
> Three queens with crowns of gold—and from them rose
> A cry that shiver'd to the tingling stars,
> And, as it were one voice, an agony
> Of lamentation, like a wind, that shrills
> All night in a waste land, where no one comes,
> Or hath come, since the making of the world.

By means of the symbolic voyage Arthur is to sail to Avilon, the island-paradise that is not too different from lotus-land. Here

> falls not hail, or rain, or any snow,
> Nor ever wind blows loudly, but it lies
> Deep-meadow'd, happy, fair with orchard-lawns
> And bowery hollows crown'd with summer sea. . . .

Avilon is the haven of refuge and regeneration: it is here, says Arthur, "Where I will heal me of my grievous wound."

In this time of crisis Bedivere thinks only of himself, seeing that he will be left alone in a hostile world where he can no longer be at ease in the old dispensation. "For now I see the true old times are dead," he says,

> And I, the last, go forth companionless.
> And the days darken round me, and the years,
> Among new men, strange faces, other minds.

The King bids him to turn his attention to faith, which accepts change, for "God fulfills himself in many ways, / Lest one good custom should corrupt the world." The times may be difficult, but difficulties can be overcome if one turns to God through prayer.

At the end of the "Morte d'Arthur" we are returned to the frame enclosing the poem. In a dream the speaker fancies himself sailing with Arthur, who comes "like a modern gentleman." The watchers on the hills cry out in greeting to the returned King and declare that "war shall be no more." At this moment the speaker is awakened by the Christmas bells. His faith in human greatness, caused by the response of the listeners to Arthur as hero, is recovered, as is his faith in the Christian tradition when he hears the church-bells on Christmas morn; and by implication he can now insist upon the validity of the epic for modern times. As in the great New Year's hymn in "In Memoriam" (CVI), the bells symbolically ring out "The faithless coldness of the times," and for the poet they "ring out my mournful rhymes" and "ring the fuller minstrel in." Here Tennyson proclaims his willingness to don the bardic mantle, and he accepts fully the concept of poetry as mission which had been tentatively hinted at in "The Palace of Art."

—Clyde de L. Ryals, *Theme and Symbol in Tennyson's Poems to 1850* (Philadelphia: Univesity of Pennsylvania Press, 1964): pp. 138–41.

[In this excerpt, Stanley J. Solomon discusses some of the tension in Tennyson's rendition of the Arthurian legend, such as the real Arthur versus a supernatural king and faith versus disbelief. Solomon sees King Arthur as a political figure questioning the value of his mission.]

An examination of *Idylls of the King* reveals that paradox, ambiguity, and irony abound in the poem. In fact, so often are entire situations built on paradoxical qualities inherent in personalities or in the society of Camelot that we must assume that Tennyson was thoroughly conscious of what he was doing. Very likely, a main source of interest to the poet was the deliberate structuring of all the events of Camelot around certain major paradoxes, most, but not all, of which are involved with his depiction of the "blameless King," who is paradoxically to blame for the destruction of his own kingdom.

In considering Arthur's character as central to the paradoxical meaning of the poem, we must first make some observations about the "realness" or humanity of the King. That Arthur does not strike all readers as a realistic character is self-evident. Indeed, many of the knights suspected that Arthur was supernatural. And Tennyson lets us know early in the *Idylls* that Arthur will stand as a symbol, not only for the reader but also for his loyal followers, who very early proclaim him in these terms: "The King will follow Christ, and we the King, / In whom high God hath breathed a secret thing" ("The Coming of Arthur," ll. 499–500). Even more indicative of the symbolic representation of the King is Bellicent's narration of the coming of Arthur—the finding of the child in the sea by Bleys and Merlin. On the other hand, Tennyson does not tell us this story directly but instead has Bellicent narrate it to Leodogran as a rumor about which she herself may have some reservations. In any case, we are not aware of widespread knowledge among the populace of Arthur's origins. The feudal barons who attempted to prevent Arthur's taking the throne believe him to be a pretender, not a supernaturally-sent leader; the knights who rally to his support do so not because of any commitments to a supra-order that they feel is to be established, but because they believe in his legitimate claims to the throne.

In fact, throughout most of the *Idylls,* Tennyson takes care to modulate the supernatural to the level of the natural. Of course, the combination of superb traits in Arthur's nature—fabulous physical adroitness, mystical insight into the divinity of the universe, complete honesty, wisdom, nobility, and innocence—is most unlikely, but such traits need not be supernatural. Until the Holy Grail incident, little occurs that is not understandable on the natural level. Analysis of Arthur's character should not bog down on the extraordinary things he accomplished. It is quite conceivable that a realistic explantion could be offered for everything that occurs with the exception of what happens in the last idyll, which is based on the myth of Arthur's passing, and which Tennyson wrote in large part many years before any of the other idylls. . . .

Perhaps in the very conception of a perfect real man there lies a paradox that cannot be resolved satisfactorily for the modern taste. Arthur is always a little stiff. While retaining the framework of the King's supernatural origin (which, though not directly stated by the poet, is never contradicted) and passing, Tennyson developed a central character who attempts to establish by example and precept the perfect state for perfect knights. Perfection is Arthur's aim, but he does not aim to destroy the "humanness" of his subjects, nor his own humanity. In other words, Tennyson is depicting a conflict between human perfectibility (which is possible because Arthur is a perfect man and not a god) confronted with human imperfectibility (which is a necessary human condition because man is not god). It is from this involved paradox that Tennyson constructs all the other central paradoxes which make up *Idylls of the King*. . . .

His kingdom in ruins, Arthur passes on to his long-anticipated immortality in Avilon, disillusioned and skeptical of the value of his own mission. Before the last battle, Sir Bedivere had heard the King, moaning in sleep, speak of what is perhaps the thematic paradox of the *Idylls:*

> 'I found Him in the shining of stars,
> I mark'd Him in the flowering of His fields,
> But in His ways with men I find Him not.
> I waged His wars, and now I pass and die.
> O me! for why is all around us here
> As if some lesser god had made the world,
> But had not the force to shape it as he would,

Till the High God behold it from beyond,
And enter it, and make it beautiful?
Or else as if the world were wholly fair,
But that these eyes of men are dense and dim,
And have not the power to see it as it is—
Perchance, because we see not to the close;—
For I, being simple, thought to work His will,
And have but stricken with the sword in vain,
And all whereon I leaned in wife and friend
Is traitor to my peace, and all my realm
Reels back into the beast, and is no more.
My God, thou has forgotten me in my death!
Nay—God my Christ—I pass but shall not die.
("The Passing of Arthur," ll. 9–28)

If Arthur could not find God in "His ways with men," then how could the King have hoped to achieve the great ideals he actually did establish, however temporarily, for his realm? Of course, this is a discouraged Arthur speaking; undoubtedly the King once though it possible to find God's ways with men. Yet in his new awareness of reality—after it has been brought home to him that Guinevere, Lancelot, and many trusted knights are not merely fallible human beings but are active sinners and traitors—Arthur does not regret having established the ideals that were at once the strength and the weakness of his kingdom.

When Arthur moans in his sleep about the mysterious ways of God and the inability of man to grasp the divine plan, he resembles the narrator of *In Memoriam,* who discovers "Nature, red in tooth and claw." But, surely, neither in the *Idylls* nor in *In Memoriam* does Tennyson suggest that one should come to grips with reality as an alternative to the mystical approach to life. From what we know of Tennyson's life, we feel that his mystical intimations might parallel Arthur's. In any case, there is much evidence in the poem itself that the alternative approach to life—the realist's approach—is absolutely certain of failure. The realist's approach is Gawain's or Tristram's, a cynical attitude with low goals, indifferent to all external verities, and dedicated only to Ruskin's Goddess of Getting-on.

Assuredly the King is unrealistic in demanding that his code of conduct be the law of the land, in expecting that men will live up to these artificial standards. Yet the paradox is that no alternative is feasible. How was Arthur to administer the country and dole out punishments and rewards if not by the creation of artificial standards of honor and trust? As Professor Buckley has stated, "the great argument of the *Idylls* as a whole is simply that, without such virtues ["self-reverence, self-knowledge, self-control"] and the faith which sanctions them, neither the individual nor the state can attain rational order or spiritual health."

Tennyson, then, demonstrates that civilization is determined by the ability of men to impose artificial (i.e., unnatural) standards on political and social relationships. The intent in promulgating these standards, in large part, is to subdue the natural (the beast) in man. The natural man is not the Christian knight but the heathen or the outlaw Earl Doorm or the rebel Red Knight. Associating the natural with wildness and lack of restraint, Arthur sees confusion and paradox in human nature leading to the total destruction of order:

> 'O Bedivere, for on my heart hath fallen
> Confusion, till I know not what I am,
> Nor whence I am, nor whether I be king;
> Behold, I seem but king among the dead.'
> ("The Passing of Arthur," ll. 143–146)

—Stanley J. Solomon, "Tennyson's Paradoxical King," *Victorian Poetry* 2, no. 4 (November 1963): pp. 259–60, 262, 267–69.

HERBERT F. TUCKER ON TENNYSON AND MALORY'S LEGACY

[Herbert F. Tucker is the author of *Browning's Beginnings: The Art of Disclosure* and *Tennyson and the Doom of Romanticism*, from which this excerpt is taken. Tucker discusses how Tennyson continues Malory's legacy, where the death of Arthur is the birth of the author. Tucker looks at the way other English literary forebears have added their own individual imprint on that legendary tradition.]

Tennyson approaches Arthurian legend in the 1830s by adopting the remarkable and drastic expedient of conceiving his theme in perennial recession from the present, and then making that recession his theme. Instead of transmitting a culturally originative tale, he tells of a culturally originative transmission. He commences to write *Idylls of the King* at the close of the story, the winter midnight that ends knightly deeds, but that also ushers in the sunrise of the new year and with it the beginning of fabulation about knightly deeds. He takes the epic plunge *in finales res* and dips into the creative matrix from which the matter of Arthur takes rise, conceived not as historical event but as traditional story. Tennyson's expanded version of this poem in the completed idylls took the title "The Passing of Arthur"—a title that beautifully identifies the moment at which a history passes into a tradition, the moment at which Arthur's passing away becomes the occasion of his being passed along as a perennially recreated cultural possession, the once and future king. But Tennyson's original title carries, as its intertextual freight, much the same implication: the death of King Arthur, which constitutes the fundamental "action" of the poem, is the birth of the "Morte d'Arthur," as it is the birth of the Arthurian miscellany which Malory set down, and to which centuries of tradition in their wisdom have given that oddly appropriate name. Tennyson's title follows Malory, and so does his text, in its narrative outline and even, where possible, in its wording; the death of Arthur being the birth of the author, Tennyson finds his secondary epic authority in high fidelity to the avowedly legendary character of what he means to transmit to modern readers. That is why, in the modernizing frame of "The Epic," Tennyson has picked from the domestic holocaust of a hypothetical twelve-book epic the one scrap needful, the coded key from which the whole story—any story that aspires to integrity in his late day—can be mapped out once again. . . .

The poem opens with the "hollow oes and aes, / Deep-chested music," promised by its frame ("The Epic," 50–51), in as handsome and efficient a piece of narrative setting as Tennyson was ever to compose:

> So all day long the noise of battle rolled
> Among the mountains by the winter sea;
> Until King Arthur's table, man by man,
> Had fallen in Lyonesse about their Lord,
> King Arthur: then, because his wound was deep,
> The bold Sir Bedivere uplifted him,
> Sir Bedivere, the last of all his knights,

And bore him to a chapel nigh the field,
A broken chancel with a broken cross,
That stood on a dark strait of barren land.
On one side lay the Ocean, and on one
Lay a great water, and the moon was full.

For Tennyson, to set a story is to set it up in imagery and theme as well as place. Although Arthur is mortally wounded, he is "uplifted" too, by a survivor, in a forecast of the governing dialectic of the poem and of its larger epic aspiration. In the aftermath of so final a battle, the chapel with its broken cross offers not socially sanctioned asylum but natural shelter; and although the only shrift or uplift awaiting the two warriors there will be what they carry in themselves, the halfway situation of the ruined holy house and the curiously expectant tranquility of the scene outside it suggest that what they carry in themselves will suffice. The physical intermediacy of the opening scene has an intertextual analogue in the opening word "So," which quickly situates this text in its tradition whether we read the word as a conjunction or as an adverb. If the former ("therefore"), it assumes the consequential force of a Greek particle, a diacritical hallmark of the classical epic. If the latter ("thus"), it allusively tells us how the noise of battle rolled; it rolled like the rhythmic periods of Malory's prose, or like the long epic line extending back from Milton to Homer.

The passage certainly accumulates a sonorous roll of its own, through aggressive alliteration and through a verbal iteration that varies the position of a repeated word or sound within or across poetic lines ("King Arthur," "chapel . . . broken chancel . . . broken cross," "On one side . . . and on one"). This verbal recycling derives within the English tradition from the example of Milton, who uses it primarily as a sophisticated elegiac keening ("For *Lycidas* is dead, dead ere his prime, / Young *Lycidas*"; 8–9), which both registers loss and proleptically whets the edge of the elegiac crisis in promise of an abundant return: "Weep no more, woeful Shepherds, weep no more" (165). This Miltonic turn of style survives through the Romantic period in the understated accumulations of Wordsworth's "Tintern Abbey" and (with special relevance to the project of "Morte d'Arthur") in the sculptural aplomb of Keats's epic fragment *Hyperion*, the first verse paragraph of which anticipates the repetitive stationing devices used by Tennyson in setting the "Morte." In one sense Tennyson's recourse to a self-returning elegiac style, here as in the early portions of the epic-bound "Oenone," signals a first stage of bereavement that the poem will undertake to transcend. But in another sense, because the transcendence Tennyson reserves for his Arthur is—even more than in the surprisingly non-Christian Malory—a mode of secular commemoration, Tennyson's register of grief also serves as an already redemptive registration of heroic names and places lost once to history but reborn in legend now again.

—Herbert F. Tucker, *Tennyson and the Doom of Romanticism* (Cambridge, Mass.: Harvard University Press, 1988): pp. 320–21, 322–24.

Works by
Alfred, Lord Tennyson

The Poetic and Dramatic Works of Alfred, Lord Tennyson, Boston and
New York: Houghtlin Mifflin & Company, 1899.

Works about
Alfred, Lord Tennyson

Abercrombie, Lascelles. *Revaluation: Studies in Biography*. Oxford: Oxford University Press, 1931.

Allen, Peter. *The Cambridge Apostles: The Early Years*. Cambridge: Cambridge University Press, 1978.

Armstrong, Isobel. *Language as Living Form in Nineteenth-Century Poetry*. Totowa, N.J.: Barnes & Noble, 1974.

Ball, Patricia. *The Central Self: A Study in Romantic and Victorian Imagination*. London: Athlone Press, 1968.

Baum, Paul F. *Tennyson Sixty Years After*. Chapel Hill: University of North Carolina Press, 1948.

Bloom, Harold. *The Ringers in the Tower: Studies in Romantic Tradition*. Chicago and London: University of Chicago Press, 1971.

Brashear, William. *The Living Will: A Study of Tennyson and Nineteenth-Century Subjectivism*. The Hague: Mouton, 1969.

Buckler, William E. *The Victorian Imagination: Essays in Aesthetic Exploration*. New York and London: New York University Press, 1980.

Buckley, Jerome H. *Tennyson: The Growth of a Poet*. Cambridge, Mass.: Harvard University Press, 1960.

Bush, Douglas. *Mythology and the Romantic Tradition in English Poetry*. Cambridge, Mass.: Harvard University Press, 1937.

Colley, Ann C. *Tennyson and Madness*. Athens, Ga.: University of Georgia Press, 1983.

Culler, A. Dwight. *The Poetry of Tennyson*. New Haven and London: Yale University Press, 1977.

Deacon, Richard. *The Cambridge Apostles*. 1985.

Dyson, Hope, and Charles Tennyson. *Dear and Honoured Lady: The Correspondence Between Queen Victoria and Alfred Tennyson*. London: Macmillan, 1969.

Foakes, R.A. *The Romantic Assertion: A Study in the Language of Nineteenth Century Poetry*. New Haven: Yale University Press, 1958.

Goslee, David F. *Tennyson's Characters: "Strange Faces, Other Minds."* Iowa City: University of Iowa, 1989.

Gransden, K.W. *Tennyson: In Memoriam.* London: Edward Arnold, 1964.

Gray, J.M. *Thro' the Vision of the Night: A Study of Source, Evolution, and Structure in Tennyson's "Idylls of the King."* Montreal: McGill-Queen's University Press, 1980.

Hair, Donald S. *Domestic and Heroic in Tennyson's Poetry.* Toronto: University of Toronto Press, 1981.

Houghton, Walter. *The Victorian Frame of Mind, 1830–1870.* New Haven: Yale University Press, 1951.

Hughes, Linda K. *The Manyfacèd Glass: Tennyson's Dramatic Monologues.* Athens: Ohio University Press, 1987.

Hungerford, Edward B. *The Shores of Darkness.* New York: Columbia University Press, 1941.

Joseph, Gerhard. *Tennysonion Love: The Strange Diagonal.* Minneapolis: University of Minnesota Press, 1969.

Jump, J.D. *Tennyson: The Critical Heritage.* London: Routledge & Kegan Paul, 1967.

Killham, John. ed. *Critical Essays on the Poetry of Tennyson.* London: Routledge and Kegan Paul, 1960.

Kincaid, James R. *Tennyson's Major Poems: The Comic and Ironic Pattern.* New Haven: Yale University Press, 1958.

Martin, Robert Bernard. *Tennyson: The Unquiet Heart.* Oxford: Clarendon Press, 1980.

Mermin, Dorothy. *The Audience in the Poem: Five Victorian Poets.* New Brunswick: Rutgers University Press, 1983.

Pattison, Robert. *Tennyson and Tradition.* Cambridge, Mass.: Harvard University Press, 1979.

Peckham, Morse. *Beyond the Tragic Vision: The Quest for Identity in the Nineteenth Century.* New York: Braziller, 1962.

———. *Victorian Revolutionaries: Speculations on Some Heroes of a Culture Crisis.* New York: Braziller, 1970.

Peltason, Timothy. *Reading "In Memoriam."* Princeton: Princeton University Press, 1985.

Pinion, F.B. *A Tennyson Companion*. New York: St. Martin's Press, 1984.

Pitt, Valerie. *Tennyson Laureate*. London: Barrie and Rockliff, 1962.

Priestley, F.E.L. *Language and Structure in Tennyson's Poetry*. London: Deutsch, 1973.

Pyre, J.F.A. *The Formation of Tennyson's Style*. Madison: University of Wisconsin Studies, 1921.

Reed, John R. *Victorian Conventions*. Athens: Ohio University Press, 1975.

Ricks, Christopher. *Tennyson*. New York: Macmillan, 1972.

Rosenberg, John D. *The Fall of Camelot: A Study of Tennyson's "Idylls of the King,"* Cambridge, Mass: Havard University Press, 1973.

Ryals, Clyde de L. *Theme and Symbol in Tennyson's Poems to 1850*. Philadelphia: University of Philadelphia Press, 1964.

Shannon, Edgar F., Jr. *Tennyson and the Reviewers: A Study of His Literary Reputation and of the Influence of the Critics upon His Poetry, 1827–1851*. Cambridge, Mass.: Harvard University Press, 1952.

Sinfield, Alan. *The Language of Tennyson's "In Memoriam."* Oxford: Blackwell, 1971.

Staines, David. *Tennyson's Camelot: The "Idylls of the King" and Its Medieval Sources*. Waterloo, Ontario: Wilfrid Laurier University Press, 1982.

Turner, Paul. *Tennyson*. London: Routledge and Kegan Paul, 1976.

Wheatcroft, Andrew. *The Tennyson Album*. London: Routledge and Kegan Paul, 1980.

Index of
Themes and Ideas